CURBING INFLATION THROUGH TAXATION

CURBING INFLATION THROUGH TAXATION

By

Marriner S. Eccles
Alvin H. Hansen
J. W. Oliver
James F. Hughes
Milton Gilbert
Roy Blough
Seth D. Sims
Carl Shoup
Homer Hoyt
S. E. Harris
Irvin Bussing
Arthur Z. Arnold
Marius Farioletti
George A. Tesoro
Godfrey N. Nelson
A. Kenneth Eaton
Alfred G. Buehler
Mary E. Murphy

Symposium conducted by the

TAX INSTITUTE

February 7-8, 1944, New York

Essay Index Reprint Series

BOOKS FOR LIBRARIES PRESS
FREEPORT, NEW YORK

Reprinted 1971 by arrangement with
the Tax Institute of America

INTERNATIONAL STANDARD BOOK NUMBER:
0-8369-2377-4

LIBRARY OF CONGRESS CATALOG CARD NUMBER:
79-128319

PRINTED IN THE UNITED STATES OF AMERICA

CONTENTS

PART FIVE

Possibilities of Postwar Inflation and Suggested Tax Action

APPENDIX

FOREWORD

So MUCH has been said about tax policy and inflation in recent months that another conference devoted to the question may seem to be superfluous. But those who are best informed are well aware that there are still many unsolved problems. Many technical matters are still in the realm of opinion. Changing conditions create new problems. And the educational job has scarcely begun.

A few years ago the fields of public and private finance were sharply divided, as were also the work of the theorists and the work of the practitioners. Today all of the knowledge and considered judgment of bankers, tax administrators, and the students of public finance and business cycles must be pooled if the best procedure is to be adopted.

Nor is it sufficient to call upon the experts. It is necessary to convince the taxpayers and the potential bond buyers of the dangers of inflation. And it is necessary for every consumer to realize that his buying will contribute to inflation, and that his saving will help to check it.

The total cost of our national government from its origin to the beginning of this war was less than 160 billion dollars. This sum is considerably less than we have spent in the brief period since the war began. If President Roosevelt's budget for 1945 is realized, we shall have spent twice as much on this war by the end of the next fiscal year as we spent in the whole span of our national history before the war began. Our annual expenditures exceed the total national income in any prewar year. Physical production—and the national income—have, of course, been enormously increased; but half of our output, or more, goes directly to war uses.

The financing of war expenditures on this scale is a Herculean task. Financing them without serious inflation requires skill of the highest order. There is some ground for congratulation on our achievements thus far. With a far more costly war than any in our preceding history, whether cost is measured in billions of dollars or as a percentage of the national product, we have covered a larger proportion of total expenditures with tax revenues. Yet the "inflationary gap" has been dangerously large.

Only a negligible part of the cost of the Revolution was met from tax revenues, since the national government had no taxing power. During the Civil War, the Confederacy derived a little more than one-tenth of its receipts from taxes, and the Union was able to cover more than one-fifth of its costs from this source. The proportion of costs covered by taxes was pushed up to one-fourth for the first World War, and to nearly one-third for the first years of the second World War (1941-42 and 1942-43). Budget figures for 1943-44 and 1944-45 raise this proportion to more than two-fifths. A substantial part of the costs of both the Revolution and the Civil War was covered by issues of paper money, some of which were never redeemed. Such issues have not been resorted to in either the first or the second World War. And this improved financing is reflected in price levels.

Fortunately, much of the surplus spending power has in fact been saved and a relatively small portion has contributed to rising prices. In view both of the possible price increases offered by this surplus income and of our experience in the first World War actual price increases have been moderate. But they have been sufficient to create genuine—and unnecessary—hardship. And in concentrating on this obvious measure there is some danger that we shall overlook other important indicators of inflation.

The index of the cost of living is not the sole test. Not all savings have gone into government bonds. And savings invested in real estate or the stock market may bring inflation. We suffered serious inflation in the nineteen-twenties without any important increases in the cost of living. Instead we had real estate booms in Iowa and Florida; and we had a stock market boom of unprecedented proportions. These are factors to watch today.

The war on inflation has yet to be won. In fact, the most critical battles will probably come after the war on the Axis is over. It is with this in mind that the subject of this year's conference of the Tax Institute was chosen. The members of the Program Committee are Mabel Newcomer, Vassar College; James W. Martin, University of Kentucky; William J. Shultz, New York State Department of Taxation and Finance; and Mabel L. Walker, Tax Institute. We hope that the exchange of information and opinions in this symposium may take us one step farther toward our goal.

MABEL NEWCOMER
Chairman,
Program Committee

Vassar College
February, 1944

PART ONE

EARMARKS OF INFLATION

CHAPTER I

CONSUMER SPENDING DURING THE WAR

MILTON GILBERT

Acting Chief, Division of Research and Statistics
Bureau of Foreign and Domestic Commerce

AFTER A FEW years' experience as a statistician, it has gradually dawned upon me that the occupation has one major drawback—a drawback very pointedly illustrated by the program of the present meeting. It is that the statistician always gets called upon in a session dealing with some vital issue of the day, to start the discussion with a bare presentation of the unadorned facts, while the exciting and controversial aspects of the question are left for more balanced minds later in the meeting. This routine not only deprives the statistician of much of the fun, but tends to develop in him an inferiority complex.

Since, however, I have noticed so great a disregard of the facts in much of the current discussion concerning inflation and taxation I am not at all unhappy about serving the function here of a statistical table.

It is necessary from the standpoint of the broader purpose of this symposium to examine the facts concerning consumer spending during the war by considering first what has happened to the flow of income, and what are the major components in the disposition of that income. The broad picture is shown in the chart on the following page. I should mention that the estimates we have presented for the year 1943 are based upon less than full-year data and consequently may be revised to some extent.

Flow of Income to Individuals

The first thing to note is that the mobilization of our economy for war has been accompanied by a tremendous increase in the flow of income to individuals. From a level of about 71 billion dollars in 1939, income payments rose to 142 billion dollars in 1943. Thus income has doubled in the course of the past four years. I begin with this because what has happened to income is, of course, the most basic factor behind what has happened to consumer spending. This rise

DISPOSITION OF INCOME PAYMENTS TO INDIVIDUALS
(SEASONALLY ADJUSTED AT ANNUAL RATE)

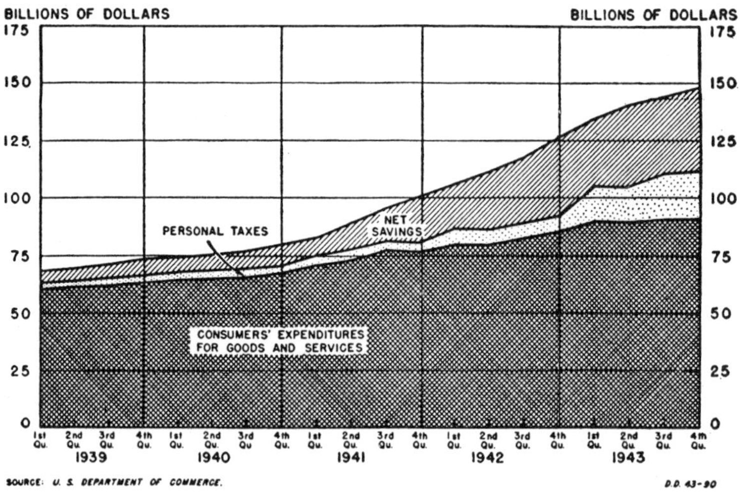

in income is in part a reflection of the inflation which has occurred during the war period, but much more important has been the increase in the utilization of the factors of production which has made our huge war output possible.

Looking now at the disposition of this enlarged flow of

income, you can see that all three of the major uses of income, that is—expenditures, savings and taxes—have risen substantially. In the case of consumer expenditures, you will note that the 1939 level of 62 billion dollars became 91 billion dollars by 1943. Personal taxes—which includes all taxes paid directly by individuals as contrasted with those which appear on the accounts of business firms—increased from 3 billion dollars to 18 billion dollars over this same period, while the net savings of individuals rose from 6 billion dollars in 1939 to the rather astounding total of 33 billion dollars in 1943. I might mention that the increase in taxes has been entirely federal since state and local personal taxes totalled approximately 2 billion dollars in both 1939 and 1943.

If we contrast the 1943 with the 1939 situation, it may be seen, therefore, that out of the increase in income of 71 billion dollars, 29 billion dollars were being spent, 15 billion were being paid in higher taxes, and 27 billion were being saved.

Consumer Expenditures During the War

To turn now to consumer spending as such, I think the available facts warrant the generalization that consumers as a whole have bought almost everything in sight, and that their demand has pressed upon the available productive capacity for virtually all types of goods and services. There have been a few notable instances in which expenditures for a major category of consumers' goods declined in the course of the war, but after one has mentioned automobiles, household appliances, and gasoline, the list of declines is just about exhausted.

I do not mean to imply, of course, that there have not been lots of minor items which have been either curtailed or eliminated, but only that these minor curtailments have not been large enough to offset the increases in expenditures for the other items within their major groups. This is apparent from the fact that total spending did increase by 29 billion dollars from 1939 to 1943.

The upward trend in consumer spending has been evident in every other major category of expenditures except the three which I mentioned—automobiles, household appliances and gasoline. To point out a few types of spending that have shown particular buoyancy, expenditures for jewelry increased 168 per cent; expenditures in eating and drinking places, 126 per cent; and expenditures for women's apparel and accessories, 121 per cent.

Our estimates of consumers' expenditures for services show a rise of about 30 per cent, and this in the face of a relatively moderate increase in rents paid which constitute a fairly sizable proportion of service expenditures as a whole. Within the services, the particularly large gains have been amusements, with an increase of 67 per cent; transportation, with a rise of 39 per cent; and personal services with an advance of 55 per cent.

Reasons for Increase in Expenditures

Now, as is well known, the increase in consumers' expenditures over the war period is partly accounted for by the rising trend of prices. In other words, consumers have increased their expenditures from 62 billion dollars in 1939 to 91 billion dollars in 1943, partly because they purchased more goods and services and partly because they paid higher prices for those goods and services.

It is extremely difficult to disentangle these two elements with precision, not only because of the inadequacies of our price information but also because the very concept of "the quantity of goods and services" is not particularly well adapted to a period during which the composition of output is drastically changed. Nevertheless, we have attempted an approximate adjustment for price changes and find that about two-thirds of the increase in expenditures over this period is accounted for by rising prices while one-third is accounted for by an increase in the quantity of goods and services received by consumers. This implies that the quantity of goods and services received by consumers increased about 15 per cent from 1939 to 1943. (I might say parenthetically that the impression of widespread shortages throughout the consumers' goods field, which many people seem to have, has been created not by an actual shrinkage in the flow of goods to consumers, but by the failure of moderately increasing supplies to meet the additional demand resulting from the huge increase in income.)

Implicit in this result is an average price rise over the entire gamut of consumers' goods and services of approximately 28 per cent. This adjustment for rising prices was made very largely on the basis of the price information collected by the Bureau of Labor Statistics covering purchases of urban workers, and the Bureau of Agricultural Economics covering purchases of farmers. The average price rise for all consumers' expenditures, however, necessarily differs from that shown by the cost-of-living indexes for urban workers or for farmers since the distribution of expenditures for the nation as a whole is different from that for either the worker or the farmer segment.

The fact that we have witnessed an increase in the flow of goods and services to consumers in the neighborhood of 15 per cent during a period in which we were mobilizing our economic resources to fight a major war has been a surprise to most observers. I think it means primarily that most of us substantially underestimated the productive capacity of our economy when fully utilized. It is not, however, without importance for the policy decisions of the coming months that we were able to achieve so high a flow of consumers' goods in 1943 only because a fairly sizable reduction in inventories of consumers' goods was feasible.

Implications of Trends

I would like to turn in conclusion to a few of the implications of the trends we have been discussing that have a bearing on present and future policy. In the first place, I think it must be concluded that in our mobilization for war we have placed only moderate reliance upon taxation as a means of controlling inflation. It was not until 1943 that personal taxes became at all substantial, and by that time the magnitude of net savings of individuals was so large that the main effect of the rise in taxes seems to have been to limit savings rather than to curtail expenditures. From this it follows that unless a tax increase at the present time is rather large, it will come mostly out of savings, leaving consumers' expenditures relatively unaffected.

The second conclusion is pointed up by the following chart showing the relationship between retail sales and disposable income—that is, income after the deduction of taxes. You will see that expenditures in nondurable goods stores have maintained a very stable relationship with disposable income throughout the entire war period. On the other hand, sales of durable goods stores have fallen far below the relationship that would have been consistent with the level of income in both 1942 and 1943. The fairly startling fact revealed by these two relationships is that for the population as a whole there has not been *any diversion* of the income released by shortages of durable goods into the nondurable goods field. A couple of years ago when we were trying to calculate the possible magnitude of the inflationary pressure, the assumption in fairly general use was that 50 per cent of the money that could not be spent on durable goods would spill

RELATIONSHIP BETWEEN SALES OF RETAIL STORES AND DISPOSABLE INCOME OF INDIVIDUALS

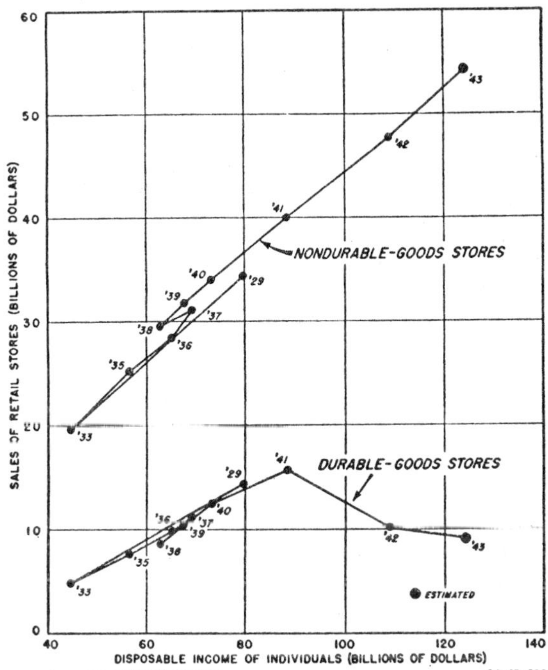

SOURCE: U.S. DEPARTMENT OF COMMERCE. D.D. 43-596

over to the nondurable goods sector. Certainly, no one that I know of would have expected *no* spill-over.

There is little doubt that the reason no such spill-over occurred has been the effectiveness of price control and rationing. This conclusion receives emphasis from the fact that in the case of some types of products where it is well known that price control has been less effective—such as women's apparel and jewelry—consumers' expenditures in the past two years have risen well above their previous relation to disposable income.

Now, the implication of this which has a direct bearing upon the arguments one hears in discussions of policy is this: savings of individuals have been so very large, partly because price control and rationing have limited the amount which the consumer has had to spend for the available supply of goods. It, therefore, seems evident that any relaxation of our direct control machinery would lead rather promptly to further inflation. The notion that the voluntary savings of individuals have been very important in filling the inflationary gap considerably overstates the case because a large part of the savings increase has not really been very voluntary.

CHAPTER II

FARM LAND BOOM

SETH D. SIMS

Assistant to the Secretary of Agriculture

THE HISTORY of this country is replete with accounts of speculative dealings in land. From the colonial days down to the present, the terms "land grabbing," "land jobbing," and "land boom" have been markings on the economic thermometer that registered the fever of land speculation. And, like the aftereffects of high body fever, exececssive land fever has almost invariably left the economic system in a weak and rundown condition.

HISTORICAL RETROSPECT

To the settlers themselves—and their royal backers across the Atlantic—this country was viewed as a speculative proposition. The land and its increments were looked upon as a source of great and quick wealth. The conveyance of unoccupied lands to private individuals or groups of individuals which undertook the management, settlement and resale, was a common practice in colonial times. Quick turnover with a large profit on as small an investment as possible has long been the established pattern of land and other types of speculation.

The great wave of excitement attending the National Land Office sales during the wild speculation just prior to the 1837 financial panic gave rise to the expression "doing a land office business," an expression which is still used to denote great commercial activity. Something of the nature of the speculative trend of the second quarter of the 19th century is indicated by the fact that receipts from public land sales in 1825 amounted to only about a million and a quarter dollars. By 1836, they had risen to over 25 million dollars, and in 1837 fell to just a little more than 7 million dollars.

From 1850 on the choice agricultural lands of the country steadily rose in value. Judged by present day standards the prices were low, but in Iowa, values in 1900 were seven times what they were in 1850. Around the turn of the century the country, so far as settlement and pioneering were concerned, could be said to be coming of age. From 1900 to 1910 there was a more rapid increase in land values throughout the entire country where crops could be readily grown.

While "land boom" was a common phenomenon in this country before 1800 and could properly be applied to happenings in different sections of the country on numerous occasions, the term did not attain full national status until the 1916-20 period during and immediately following World War I. Its full significance to the national economy was not understood for another fifteen years after that.

Case History of an Iowa Farm

To show what can happen when a piece of land becomes involved in speculative transactions, let's take a look at what has happened to one Iowa farm tract of 160 acres from 1884 to the present time. This carries one farm, which is typical of thousands of others, through the biggest land boom the country has ever seen—during World War I and immediately following—through the depression period and now well into what gives all indication of another real boom.

Previous to 1884, this land had been sold four times as a

part of an 800-acre tract. In all four sales the price was $10 an acre or less. This 160-acre tract did not change hands between 1884 and 1909. In 1909, it changed hands at $100 an acre and was mortgaged for $10,000. Between 1909 and 1916 it was sold twice, in 1913 at $145 an acre and in 1914 at $151 an acre. The next sale, in 1916—when World War I boom was just ahead—was for $188 an acre. A $20,000 mortgage was given in part payment. In 1917, the owner purchased 80 additional acres—unimproved—for which he paid $190 an acre on which a mortgage of $13,700 was given. Then, in 1920 the 240 acres sold at the amazing figure of $396 per acre. The new owner mortgaged the land for $45,700, and raised the balance of the $95,000 required by mortgaging the 310-acre farm he had previously owned and operated for $49,000. This farm was free of encumbrance before his new purchase.

Foreclosure in 1927 took first the 80 acres added in 1917. In 1928 the original 160 acres were lost also by foreclosure. That 160 was sold again in 1930 at $170 an acre, a $15,900 mortgage being given as part payment. By 1933 the man who had purchased in 1930 had to take advantage of the foreclosure moratorium because he was unable to pay interest on the debt of approximately $110 per acre. Two years later the owner came out from under the moratorium. That 160-acre plot is now about to undergo the seventh transfer at a price of $200 per acre. In fact, it was sold for $200 in 1943 but the owner backed out of the sale and was sued by the "purchaser." Local people at present value the farm at $200 to $235 an acre. The chief loser was the farmer who had a good 310-acre farm free of debt on which he borrowed $49,000 to make a purchase of another 240 acres. He lost this original farm by foreclosure in 1933 after 13 years of a losing battle against an unsurmountable debt.

SALE AND MORTGAGE HISTORY OF IOWA FARM

Year	Acres	Owner	Sale Price		Mortgages			Mortgagee
			Total	Per Acre	Total	Per Acre	No.	
1909	160	A to B	$16,000	$100	$10,000	$ 62	1	A
1913	160	B to C	23,000	145	14,000	87	2	A $10,000; mortgage company, $4,000
1914	160	C to D	24,230	151	14,000	87	2	A and mortgage co.
1916	160	D to E	30,000	188	20,000	125	2	A $10,000 and D $10,000
1917	80	X to E	15,200	190	13,700	171	1	X—$13,700
	240	E	45,200	189	33,700	140	3	
1920	240	E to F	95,000	396	45,700	190	3	X—$13,700 on 80 acres; Ins. Co. $16,000 on 160; E—2d $16,000 on 160
*1920	310	F	...	....	49,000	158	2	Ins. Co. $27,000 Bank $22,000
FORECLOSURE								
1927	80	F to {X Sheriff E &			$15,103			
1928	160	F to Bank			19,197 (2d mortgage)			
*1933	310	F to Ins. Co.			34,000 (1st mortgage only)			
SALE BY BANK								
1930	160	Bank–G	$27,200	$170	$15,900	$99		Ins. $14,400 2d—Priv. $1,500
MORATORIUM								
1933	160	G	......	....	$17,600	$110		
1935	160	G	......	....	Out from moratorium			
1939	160	G	......	....	13,500	84.37		
1943	160	G	......	....	8,000	50		
1943	160	G to H	$32,000	$200	......	....		

* 310-acre farm owned clear by F before he purchased 240 acres from E.

Source: Data for this table and information relating to it from W. G. Murray of Iowa State College.

Behind that example lies the heartbreak, loss of dignity, and suffering caused by people paying too much for land. During part of that period when it was taking all the money the owner could scrape together to try to meet the interest payments, the buildings were allowed to depreciate seriously, and no doubt his family were deprived of many of the necessities of life simply because they were putting all of the dollars and cents they could rake and scrape together into a bad bargain.

Since World War I there has been developed by farm land appraisers a "normal" valuation appraisal. The normal valuation is one based on the long-time earning capacity of the land based on average yields for the particular farm and estimated average normal prices for farm products expected to prevail for a period of years in the future. Costs of labor and machinery and other production costs are considered as well. A reasonable return is figured on investment. It is interesting to note that a normal valuation on this farm whose history I have just given you is $135 per acre. May I add that our Farm Credit Administration employs only normal valuation appraisals in making loans to farmers. A number of the leading insurance companies who invest funds in farm mortgages also follow essentially this plan.

A large part of the trouble in boom times comes from second, third, fourth, and even lower order mortgages taken by successive owners of a farm before the bubble bursts.

Land Boom Following World War I

Let's look for a moment at the general situation in the last land boom—the one which accompanied and followed World War I, and the one that hit an all-time high in land-boom history. After that inflationary land spree hit its height in 1919-20 and prices turned downhill, land values were on the downgrade for 13 long years. The slope was steep from 1920 to '24 and fairly gentle from '24 to '30, but again steeper than ever from '30 to '33.

But this ill-fated ride that land values took doesn't tell the real story of what happened to literally hundreds of thousands of people involved in that terrific plunge that ended so disastrously for them. In 1921 farmers and "investors" began losing their farms in mounting numbers. Estimates have placed the number of farms and tracts lost by forced sale since 1920 at more than 2 milion. This means that the equivalent of one-fourth to one-third of all land in farms has gone through forced sales in the last 22 years. The great bulk of these involuntary transfers had as their chief cause an initial mistake of a man's paying too much for land.

As a result of the experience of the decade and a half following the land boom of 1919-20, the phenomena associated with a deflation of farm land prices are fairly well known. But less generally known are some of the features of the boom itself. I use Iowa again to illustrate my point. I cite what happened in Iowa because it was the center of the midwestern boom of 1919-20, and because fewer and less satisfactory data are available for other states.

The value per acre of improved farm land in Iowa increased 122 per cent from 1900 to 1910; and then, from this already high level of 1910, a further rise of 137 per cent occurred by 1920.

At the peak of the boom in 1919, the volume of transfers was more than twice the 1910-14 prewar average.[1] Of the farm sales during the first eight months in 1919 in the 60 counties surveyed at that time, almost exactly one-third involved farms sold more than once during the period and 7 per cent in-

[1] Data on 1919-20 Iowa land boom drawn chiefly from *Farm Land Values in Iowa,* by L. C. Gray and O. G. Floyd. U. S. Department of Agriculture Bulletin 874, 1920.

volved farms sold more than twice. A number of instances are reported of farms having been sold five and six times during the period.

Many people who otherwise would not have been interested in the land market bought for the purpose of selling again within a short time. The motive was not for investment and had little reference to the earning power of the land except insofar as this might form a basis for judging the probability of further increase of value. This class of buyers greatly increased the volume of demand for farm land. Moreover, since most of this class also desired to sell again as soon as a substantial speculative profit could be realized, the volume of supply was considerably increased. About one-fourth of the purchases were made with the definite intent to resell at a higher price. Over one-fifth of the sellers sold in order to buy other land. An additional one-third sold to realize a speculative profit. And, of course, the professional land dealers figured prominently in the matter of adding to the excitement and increasing the activity.

Figures show that 69 per cent of the realized gain went to town and city people and 31 per cent to dwellers in the country. Also, the data indicate that almost three-fourths of the sales were effected through an agent, and the total boomtime "take" by real estate men in commissions alone was estimated at 3 million dollars.

Danger Signals in Present Situation

What we should be concerned about now is doing all we can to prevent a repetition of that dangerous experience in this war. Already the danger signals are out. Another serious land boom seems to be in the making. The rate at which land prices are rising is greater than in the corresponding time of World War I—in many localities it is rising faster than ever before. The volume of sales in 1943 was greater than in the record year 1919, and the number of resales in certain areas point unmistakably toward a speculative land spree unless it is headed off in some way.

Now let's look for a moment at some of the factors which are contributing to the present land boom. First, it is significant to note that demand deposits of representative country banks are about three times what they were five years ago, and double what they were at the time of Pearl Harbor. Add to that the increased purchasing power of people in cities, who might want to invest in farm land, and the result is a terrific amount of money that could be used to bid up land prices. This huge backlog of surplus funds is exerting a tremendous amount of pressure, not only on land prices, but on prices in general. This situation is aggravated by a boom psychology such as occurred frequently in other periods of our history. The "boomers" are already busy; the rapid rise of land prices is too much for many people with a little extra money to spend.

A great many seem to have the notion as in the last boom that since farm commodities are bringing good prices and since the demand is stronger than it has ever been in history—times will always be like this. They overlook the possibility of having to meet high payments in a period when prices may not be so favorable—they forget that it normally takes a long time to pay for a farm. Some people who are not farmers feel that there is a certain amount of security about having a piece of land in their name, regardless of the price they pay, in these times—without giving thought to the possibility that the very purchase of land at inflationary prices may do as much or more than anything else to undermine their future security as well as the future security of the community in which they live.

Even in the face of a highly inflated land market, there are those persons who are complacent simply because they themselves aren't buying any of the high-priced land. When deflation hits, however, and the land that was purchased at prices that were too high goes on the auction block, taxes can't be paid, bonds go in default, banks close. It is inevitable that the whole community and everybody in it suffers.

It may be hard for some people to believe that a land boom of serious proportions is already underway, because from their limited observation they haven't yet seen wholesale transfers of land. These persons do not realize that it takes the transfer of only a relatively small percentage of the total number of farms in a community at inflationary prices to set off an inflationary spiral. Price levels of farms in a locality at a time like this, or any other time, are set or changed by the sales made even though they may be few in number; they are determined by the demand for farm land. If that demand is supported by a speculative fever or boom psychology to any appreciable extent, a runaway market is inevitable.

It would be difficult to determine what percentage of a market must be speculative before a "boom" results but it is safe to say that fluctuations in land prices would be materially reduced if the possibility of speculative profits were largely removed. Wild fluctuations would be absent and little economic disturbance would result if reasonable operating income probabilities plus the value of the farm as a home represented the total or even the major purchase motivations of all purchasers.

Curbing Boom by Tax On Speculative Gains

In conclusion, I should like to discuss briefly the Farm Land Boom Profits Tax Bill which has been introduced in Congress by Senator Gillette of Iowa. The Department of

Agriculture has studied many suggested ways of heading off the land boom that is now underway. The Department has discussed the various methods with officials of the farm organizations, with real estate operators, and other departments of the government. After all of these consultations, it is the conclusion of the Department of Agriculture that a stiff tax on speculative gains offers the best single remedy.

One of the outstanding features of the proposed bill is that it affects only the speculator; but it hits him hard. It doesn't hurt the person who now has a farm and wants to sell it. Neither does it penalize the person who wants to buy a farm for a home. It will not affect the young man who comes home after the war who wants to buy a farm and settle down on it. As a matter of fact, it protects him since he will not have to pay such a high price because a lot of speculators have run up the price of land. This bill, if enacted, would require speculators to pay a tax of 90 per cent of the profits they make if they buy land and sell it before the end of two years. Each year after that, the tax would decrease until it runs out at the end of six years.

It is not claimed that such a measure in itself would completely control land prices, but it would go a long way toward stopping the type and scale of speculation which has contributed more than is generally realized to our booms of the past.

CHAPTER III

INFLATION IN URBAN LAND IN WORLD WAR II

HOMER HOYT

Director of Economic Studies, Regional Plan Association, New York City

INFLATION in urban real estate does not necessarily coincide with inflation in farm real estate. During World War 1, the prices of urban real estate remained almost stationary, while the sales value of American farm land doubled between 1910 and 1920. Then when the sales value of urban land in American cities, with a population of 30,000 or over, rose from 25 to 50 billion dollars from 1920 to 1926, the value of all farm land dropped from 55 billion dollars to 37 billion dollars. The cause of this remarkable reversal in the relative position of urban and agricultural real estate was the decline in farm prices at the very time when there was a great migration of workers to the cities, which were enjoying a postwar industrial boom.

CONSEQUENCES OF URBAN LAND INFLATION

Urban real estate is still suffering from the collapse that followed the land boom of the 1920's which was based upon extravagant hopes of a continued rapid rate of urban population growth and a concentration of that growth upon limited central areas.

Since the value of most urban plots depends upon the net

yield that can be obtained by erecting buildings upon the sites, it is necessary to analyze recent trends in the sales of improved properties to determine the probable future course of prices for unimproved urban land. Nearly all urban land booms have been preceded by a rise in the net income and the sales prices of existing buildings which stimulated new building, and which, in turn, created a demand for land for building sites. This sudden increase in the rate of absorption of land by buildings frequently led to expectations of a continuation of the peak rate of building at profitable rents for an indefinite period. The land boom had barely reached its top, however, before the feverish rate of new building had produced an oversupply of houses, apartments, stores, hotels and offices, with the result that rents would fall sharply and new construction, being no longer profitable, would almost cease. The demand for land for building purposes would then also fall to a very low level, and all the extravagant hopes of high net incomes from the land would collapse like a house of cards.

This inevitable deflation in these false hopes as to the income that could be realized from urban land, would not have such disastrous social consequences if the effect were confined to the land owners. Unfortunately, however, banks and insurance companies made loans on the inflated values so that the safety of the deposits was jeopardized by the decline and, still more unfortunately, cities raised the assessed values of urban land to the high points reached by false speculative hopes and some New York cities virtually pegged their assessments at that artificial level. As these cities rely for most of their revenue upon real estate taxes, and as there is a constitutional tax limitation on the tax rate, they must either maintain that these false values are justified or else seek new sources of revenue. Hence, inflation in urban land value, beyond its real long-time earning power, has had far-reaching consequences upon municipal finance.

The evil consequences of inflation of urban land extends to the suburbs, where a great many families not only lose their nest eggs in buying vacant lots that cannot be built upon for at least a decade to come, if ever, but the land is frequently blighted by being cut up into narrow lots and rendered useless either for agriculture or home sites. It is usually almost impossible to assemble the lots in these premature subdivisions into one ownership so that the land can be turned back into a farm or replatted into a new subdivision that is suitably designed for modern homesites. Hence, the mania of lot speculation not only leads to a loss of capital by the small investor, but it causes more or less permanent blighting of large tracts of land on the edge of cities. I think most of us will agree that undue inflation of urban land is an evil from many points of view. Now let us examine the extent to which inflation in land has occurred in World War II.

Rents and Prices of Improved Real Estate

It is difficult to make generalizations concerning anything as heterogeneous as urban real estate in the United States. Trends vary as between different types of property, such as single-family homes, apartments, retail stores, office buildings and factories, and as between different localities. Certain factors have affected nearly all urban real estate in the United States. Two of these forces operating as a vise would seem to be sufficient to put a damper on any inflationary trend in residential real estate. These are rent control on the one hand, which has frozen residential rents at a national average of 8 per cent above the 1939 level, and rising real estate taxes and operating costs which tend to reduce net income. Only the favorable factor of almost 100 per cent occupancy of residential quarters in most cities has partially overcome the grave disadvantage of a fixed ceiling on income with a rising trend in operating costs. Real estate taxes in New York cities have increased five- or six-fold since 1910 and real estate tax rates everywhere seem to be increasing constantly. It may be a matter of surprise to learn, therefore, that the prices of homes and apartments have been rising during the war notwithstanding these handicaps.

Real estate brokers in 287 cities report an average rise of 12 per cent in real estate prices in 92 per cent of the cities in the past two years. In Chicago, Mr. Max Fuhrer, a prominent appraiser and architect, estimates that the market price of apartment buildings there has increased from $450-$550 a room as of 1935 and 1936, to $650-$750 a room as of the middle of 1943, with further increases of 10 to 15 per cent by January, 1944. In New York a rising trend in prices of apartments is reported, notwithstanding rent control. Mr. K. S. Keyes reports that Miami apartment and hotel prices have increased 25 to 33 1/3 per cent in the last two or three years. The motivation inducing these purchases appears to be the prospect of higher rents after the war, when rent control is removed and higher construction costs will make it impossible to duplicate existing buildings at today's selling prices. The availability for investment of large sums of savings, already amounting to an estimated national total of over 50 billion dollars, and the fear of inflation may be contributing factors.

The rise in the price of 50 per cent in the prices of medium-sized single-family homes since 1935 in Chicago, and a rise in prices amounting to as much as 40 per cent since 1941 in many war cities, has been due partly to the inability to build a new house or to rent an old one. Many families were forced to buy homes because they could secure a house in no other way. The OPA requirement of a 33 1/3 per cent down payment, which was later reduced to 20 per cent, as a prerequisite to dispossessing a tenant did not apply to houses occupied by owners who were in a position to realize substantial profits in houses bought within the last seven or eight years.

Substantial price advances have also taken place in some of the resort areas. The prices of homes in Miami in the $5,000 to $7,000 class, and in Miami Beach in the $10,000 to $12,000 class, have increased 25 to 30 per cent in the last two years. At the same time, homes in areas with few war contracts or large mansions designed for the well-to-do have even declined in selling prices because of the difficulty in securing servants and the high income taxes which curtailed the amount even the wealthy have to spend for household expense. In Miami the prices of $20,000 to $30,000 homes have advanced only 10 per cent in the last year while the largest homes and estates are selling for 25 to 40 per cent less than a year ago.

All except the best located retail store properties have no ready market in many cities due to increasing store vacancies as a result of lack of merchandise and rationing difficulties. Outlying store properties in the Miami area have declined 10 to 15 per cent or more in the last two years but the sale prices of downtown business properties have increased 10 to 20 per cent in the last several years.

Office buildings in most cities are enjoying the highest occupancy ratio since 1929 and not being subject to rent control, office building managers are raising rents.

The greatest peak of factory production in the history of the United States, as a result of the demands of war, has filled most industrial space and loft buildings and caused rises in rents, notwithstanding the building of 17 billion dollars worth of war factories by the federal government.

PRICES OF VACANT URBAN LAND

What is the effect of these trends in the rents and prices of improved real estate upon the prices of vacant urban land? So far there has been no pronounced inflationary trend in urban sites. Near the edge of some cities, as in Long Island, N. Y., prices of land have been rising in anticipation of the postwar demand for homesites. In the Miami area vacant land was relatively inactive until the last few months and is now beginning to sell at prices approximately the same as those prevailing three years ago. There is an attempt to revive the sale of lots for postwar homesites with some degree of success in a number of cities. Most purchases of vacant land have been for purposes of improvement and not for speculation.

Taken as a whole, there has been only a slight, if any, increase in total urban land values. In fact, for a number of reasons very little appreciation could be expected. In Manhattan and other parts of New York City, assessed values of land have not yet been deflated from the fictitious peak selling prices of the 1920's. In most cities, the memory of the collapse of urban land values after 1929 still lingers. A new crop of land buyers does not come on the scene as quickly as a new crop of stock speculators. It takes a generation to forget a drastic real estate debacle like that from 1929 to 1932. More important, however, the prices of improved properties do not yet justify new buildings. Since an average increase of 30 per cent in construction costs since 1939 has kept pace with any advancing prices of improved real estate, apartments, stores, office buildings and hotels are still selling in many cities at prices below the reproduction cost of the building less depreciation leaving no net income for the land. With the prospect of the competition of huge factories, built by the federal government, competing with existing industrial space, with vacancies in office buildings likely to increase with the curtailment of governmental war agencies, with some war centers overbuilt with temporary housing, and with large existing store vacancies in many cities, there is not the pressing demand for new office, store, or factory buildings yielding profitable rents that will absorb land at a rapid rate and lead to a land boom.

Reasons for Not Expecting Postwar Boom

There are also even more fundamental reasons for not expecting the urban land boom of the 1920's to be repeated after this war. First, the nation's rate of population growth and, particularly the rate of urban population growth, is tapering off and that fact has been given such wide publicity that it is generally recognized. Hence, a boom cannot be so easily generated on the premise of an ever-expanding population.

Second, while there will probably be a large volume of suburban home building after the war, the area available for urban expansion has been increased in geometrical proportion by the automobile and may be still further expanded by the commuting plane. Within a total radius of 50 miles from the center of any metropolis, there is a supply of land far in excess of the needs of even a fairly rapidly growing urban center and hence the prices of most of that land cannot be subject to monopoly control. Instead of being tied down to bands within a half mile of fixed transportation routes, builders can develop almost any farm near auto highways. If express highways are built through the crowded sections of cities where traffic proceeds at a snail's pace because of congestion so that the car owner can reach the edge of the city quickly, he can speed for miles into an open country where the area in successive concentric circles increases with the square of the radius from the center of the city. As the ever-expanding urban fringe draws people from the center of the city, land values and building densities will be reduced there also.

A stationary or slow growing urban population cannot continue to form a congested mass at the center and also disperse over the commuting area. If decentralization continues, as seems probable, central areas will continue to lose population and land values will continue to fall. This will be altogether desirable from a social and city rebuilding standpoint as it will make possible building at lower densities, with more light and air for rooms, with more park and recreation space and with more of the amenities of the country within the city.

It seems to me that even without any further controls there will be no runaway inflation in vacant urban land comparable to that which took place in some American cities in 1836, 1852 to 1855, 1869 to 1873, 1887 to 1890 and 1922 to 1925. Rent control, which is by far the most effective form of price control because it is enforced by the tenants and by drastic criminal penalties, is the most drastic regulation possible for discouraging price increases in residential properties. It will be necessary to remove rent control after the war, if there is to be any substantial amount of new building by private enterprise, because construction costs, together with all prices, will probably be higher and rents in new buildings must be higher to make it profitable to build. If the differential in rents between the old and new buildings is too great, most tenants will not move but remain where they are under the rent ceiling and hence there will be scant demand for new apartments.

The removal of rent control, however, probably will not usher in any extraordinary degree of land speculation because of the competition of numerous sites opened up by the automobiles with unrationed gas. Because of the intensity of land use in the case of apartments, there are many competing sites available for these structures near fast transportation routes in most cities. Land prices will undoubtedly advance materially in areas with unusual advantages, such as, sites adjacent to subway stations and suburban lands adjoining built-up communities, and there will be widespread increases in the prices of large tracts on the edge of cities, but as most of these purchases will be for actual use, rather than for speculation, the evils of a wild land boom will probably be avoided.

Need for Subdivision Control

The greatest immediate need for control is in the field of subdivisions on the suburban fringe. The first postwar building boom will probably take place in the open country just beyond present metropolitan centers. There will be some unavoidable speculation in large tracts suitable for residential developments, but the evils of selling vacant lots to small investors, should be curbed by requiring subdividers to install all street improvements before recording their plats and by the refusal of the lending agencies and the Federal Housing Administration to allow an excessive margin between the square foot price paid for a farm and the square foot price of a raw lot for a homesite on that same farm. It is difficult to accomplish this objective in areas surrounding most cities, but it is highly important that the attempt be made to secure united action from all county and suburban town authorities because the future form of the periphery of our cities will be largely determined by the design and layout of these new developments. Subdivisions, designed solely for the purpose of making a big profit from the sale of small lots to uninformed buyers, are not likely to provide ideal homesites and will frequently merely blight large areas of land. Control of vacant lot sales by requiring subdividers to install improvements at their own expense as a prerequisite to recording their plats, might well serve as an instrument to prevent the waste of one of our greatest community assets—the belt of vacant land encircling our great cities.

CHAPTER IV

INCREASE IN BANK DEPOSITS AND MONEY IN CIRCULATION DURING THE WAR

IRVIN BUSSING

Director of Economic Research, Savings Banks Trust Company, New York

THE TOTAL circulating medium in the United States today amounts to approximately $900 per capita. This compares with $400 in May, 1920, and about $490 in December, 1929.

Total circulating medium or means of payment, as I am using the term, includes total demand and time deposits in all banks in the United States and the total amount of paper money and coin in use, excluding that held by the Treasury, Federal Reserve Banks, and Federal Reserve agents. Government deposits in war loan accounts are included but uncollected items (float) and inter-bank deposits are omitted.

INCREASE IN CIRCULATION

By taking the figures for *all* banks of all types, wherever located, we include deposits held by country banks where during the war the rate of increase has been somewhat greater than among city banks generally, as a result of the decentralizing effect of war production and the increased income of farmers. I include time deposits because for all practical purposes such deposits are liquid.

Paper money and coin amounts to about 17 per cent of the total circulating medium today as compared with 12 per cent in May, 1920, and 7.6 per cent in December, 1929.

The actual dollar amount of paper money and coin in circulation was $39 per capita in 1929, $60 in 1940 and today it is about $150 per capita—nearly four times that of 1929.

Some of the factors responsible for this increase, discussed by various writers, may be briefly enumerated here as follows:

1. Reduction of bank facilities in the early 1930's.
2. Increased hoarding resulting from banking troubles of the period.
3. Service charges on checking accounts and elimination of interest on demand balances.
4. Influx of refugee money from Europe, much of which went into strong boxes.
5. War production wages to many individuals who are not accustomed to maintaining bank accounts, plus the fact that banking facilities are not always available at war production centers.
6. The work-force today is highly mobile.
7. Gains in retail trade, especially in the nondurable goods field where most transactions are financed with cash.
8. The armed forces keep their funds in cash.
9. Cash reserves are built up by many individuals to pay taxes and buy war bonds.
10. Operators of black markets avoid records as much as possible, including bank accounts.

Great as the increase in currency circulation has been in the United States during the war, however, it has been equally great in Canada and England.

The rate of increase has been *least* in the Boston, New York, Chicago, and Minneapolis Federal Reserve Districts; and *greatest* in the Richmond, Atlanta, St. Louis, Dallas, and San Francisco Federal Reserve Districts.

Velocity of Circulation

The velocity with which the means of payment circulate is fully as important as its volume. In May, 1920, the velocity of circulation in 101 cities of the United States, excluding New York City, was about 42 times per annum; in December,

1929, 43 times, and in January, 1944, about 18.5 times. If we combine the volume of currency in its broadest sense with velocity we find that the amount is almost identical today with that of May, 1920. That is, multiplying the total volume of currency and bank deposits on a per capita basis by velocity, the product is practically the same today as in 1920. On the same basis of comparison the volume was 23 per cent greater in 1929 than today or 1920.

This means, in other words, that a million dollars did about 42 million dollars' worth of business in 1920 (velocity 42 times per year) whereas today a million dollars is doing only about 18.5 million dollars' worth of business per year. In 1920, however, the cost of living was about 15 per cent above that of January, 1944, and therefore a dollar had to do 15 per cent more work. In 1929 the price level was almost 2 per cent less than it is today and to this extent a dollar had to do less work.

One of the most important reasons for the lower velocity of circulation today is the short-circuit operations of a wartime economy. When the government does most of the buying it excludes many intermediate steps in the process of production from raw material to finished product. The government is maintaining large balances at banks in war loan accounts also and this reduces velocity. Another factor is the reduced consumption of durable consumers goods for reasons which are obvious. On the other hand, all through the 1930's the rate of circulation was at a low velocity as compared with earlier years.

In addition to the types of circulating medium thus far discussed, the public acquired about 16 billion dollars of Series E bonds to the end of 1943 (and 7.8 billion dollars of F and G bonds, in addition) which, because they are for all practical purposes demand obligations, are almost as liquid as bank deposits and cash. We may assume that if any development occurred to cause the public to convert its available cash and deposits to goods, substantial portions of these government obligations would be converted to cash also. Toward the end of 1942 the redemption ratio was about $3 per $1,000 of bonds in the hands of the public, but at the end of 1943 the rate was $6.50 per $1,000.

Slackening of Expansionist Influences

On the other hand, most signs point to a slackening of expansionist influences in the months ahead. Bank deposits and currency in circulation increased about 19.5 billion dollars in 1943 as compared with 21.5 billion in 1942, or a decrease in the rate of growth of 10 per cent. The three principal causes for larger payrolls are disappearing. Professor Slichter in the February *Atlantic Monthly* points out that ". . . the work-force is no longer growing; hours of work are not increasing; and the large movement from low paying industries into high paying industries is virtually over." This does not mean that the volume of circulating medium will decrease. It will increase as long as the level of taxation leaves a margin in the hands of the public. But the *rate* of increase will continue to decline in coming months.

Nevertheless, even though the expansionist influences are tapering off, so large a volume of purchasing power, actual and potential, has been injected into the blood stream of the community that a large-scale upward movement of prices could get under way if the public began to show a pronounced preference for goods over money.

Summary

All this boils down to the following five points:

1. *Total means of payment* today are more than double the amount

in existence in 1920 and nearly double the amount as of December, 1929 on a per capita basis, the figure today being about $900 per person.

2. *Paper money and coin* in circulation (which is included in the $900 figure just given) amounts almost to four times the 1929 figure, or $150 per capita today.

3. *Velocity of circulation* has reached an all-time low, continuing a trend in wartime which had established itself in the 1930's, but for somewhat different reasons.

4. *The "effective" volume of the means of payment* today is almost identical with that of 1920; it is 19 per cent less than in December, 1929. ("Effective" volume = the absolute amount of the means of payment × velocity.)

If the 1929 velocity returned, the effective volume would be more than double that of 1929, which incidentally might be necessary to support a national income double that of 1929, which is one of our postwar goals.

5. The apple cart could be rudely upset, however, if the velocity began to increase before the supply of consumption goods, and if the absolute volume of the means of payment was further increased by the premature redemption of war bonds on a large scale.

PART TWO

INFLATIONARY POTENTIALITIES OF THE PUBLIC DEBT

CHAPTER V

INFLATIONARY POTENTIALITIES OF THE PUBLIC DEBT

ALVIN H. HANSEN

Harvard University

A DISCUSSION of this subject requires, I think, first of all some clarification of terms. "Inflation" is a somewhat elusive word for the reason that it seems to mean all manner of things to different individuals. In particular, there is confusion frequently between what is called *monetary* inflation and *price* inflation. Monetary inflation simply means an increase in the money supply, while price inflation means to some a general increase in the cost of living and to others an increase in the price level of commodities generally. I think there would be a distinct gain if, instead of the term monetary inflation, we simply used the phrase "an expansion of the money supply," thereby reserving the term inflation entirely to substantial increases in the cost of living or of the general commodity price level.

An expansion in the money supply (monetary expansion) does not necessarily result in a price inflation. The notion, still superficially adhered to by some, that monetary expansion and price inflation are inevitably linked together, is a hangover from a crude quantity theory of money. And by money I here mean not merely currency but also demand deposits.

In what follows, it should be understood that "inflation"

and "inflationary potentialities" refer to price inflation and potential factors leading to price inflation.

Inflationary Potentialities Involved in Debt Creation

In discussing the inflationary potentialities of the public debt, I think it is of the utmost importance to distinguish very clearly two quite separate aspects of the problem. The first relates to the inflationary potentialities involved in the flow of expenditures not covered by taxes or, in other words, in the *process* of debt creation; the second relates to the inflationary or deflationary implications involved in the existence of a public debt already created. Let us consider these two aspects of the problem in order.

With respect to the first problem—the effect of a flow of expenditures in excess of tax collections involving an increase in the public debt—not infrequently quite superficial and erroneous conclusions have been reached. It has sometimes been asserted that an increase in the public debt, ipso facto, will produce both a monetary expansion and a price inflation.

Let it be noted to begin with that the process of government borrowing need indeed not increase the quantity of money (currency and demand deposits). If the government borrows from individuals who draw upon their demand deposits when paying for the bonds, it is clear that no increase in deposits occurs—merely a transfer of existing deposits from individuals to the government. Only in the event that the individuals borrow from the banks in order to purchase government bonds, or in the event that the banks themselves purchase government bonds, will the volume of deposits rise.

A rise in the volume of deposits need not, however, affect the cost of living or the general level of prices. The newly created deposits will be used by the government to finance its expenditures and will be transferred to private corporations and individuals. These in turn may hold the deposits idle or, in other words, as a liquid asset available for future tax payment or for postwar reconversion. Clearly, we are interested not in the quantity of currency and demand deposits, but rather in the flow of expenditures, public and private.

Government borrowing means, of course, government expenditures in excess of those financed from taxes. An increase of expenditures financed from taxes may be offset by a decline in private expenditures. On the other hand, an increase in expenditures financed by borrowing may also more or less deter private expenditures, especially when borrowed from the public. An increase in public expenditures financed by borrowing from banks is likely to deter private expenditures little if at all. Thus, expenditures financed by borrowing may or may not, according to circumstances, result in an increase in total expenditures, public and private, or, in other words, in an increase in the flow of money income.

An increase of total expenditures, public and private, may or may not produce a price inflation. An increase in total expenditures will, of course, result in a general increase in the effective demand for goods and services. But, if one starts with a condition of unused resources, an increase in effective demand all around will, for the most part, result in an increase in employment and output without an increase in prices. With respect to commodities for which the output cannot easily increase, prices will tend to rise long before full employment is reached. This applies particularly to agricultural commodities. It is for this reason that in general any increase in employment in the urban communities will quickly reflect itself in an increase in agricultural prices.

Such increase may, however, more correctly be referred to as a reflation of prices that have fallen unduly low owing to the depressed state of business activity in the urban communities.

Thus, it is only at the condition of substantially full employment that an increase in effective demand leads us squarely up against the problem of inflation. It is true that an economy undergoing a drastic conversion from peace to war will experience, in many areas, bottlenecks long before the problem of general price inflation is reached. In a peacetime economy, with no drastic conversion problems, one should scarcely expect to find serious bottlenecks.

An increase in public borrowing, so long as there is widespread unemployment, offers no dangerous inflationary potentialities. In wartime, however, the point of full employment must fairly soon be reached. Beyond that point any increase in public expenditures must be offset by a decrease in private expenditures if inflation is to be prevented. This offsetting effect can, of course, most easily be achieved if the increase in government expenditures is financed by taxes. But some considerable reduction of private expenditures may be accomplished by borrowing from the public. Borrowing from the banks can, of itself, clearly induce no offsetting decline in private expenditures. This type of borrowing, therefore, has the greatest inflationary potentialities.

Since in fact all modern governments have found it politically necessary to finance a very large fraction of war expenditures by borrowing from banks, inflationary potentialities appear. But these potentialities need not result in price inflation. Private expenditures may be curtailed as an offset to the increase in public expenditures even though holdings of currency and demand deposits increase. No inconsiderable part of this restraint in private expenditures is voluntary. If you cannot buy an automobile, you may decide not to spend at all. If you cannot build a house, you may decide to save your money in order to build after the war. In part, the voluntary restraint on spending is induced by fears or anticipations with respect to the future—the fear of future tax increases, the fear of future unemployment, anticipations with respect to postwar business needs, and so on. Private expenditures have in fact also been sharply curtailed in all the warring countries by a program of rationing which indeed, under conditions of scarcity, is a necessary counterpart of a general program of price control. The success of these measures in this country thus far exceeds, I believe, the expectations of everyone. Let us not forget that back in 1940 it was widely believed that a program of general price control could not succeed in this country. The success up to date may indeed be set down as a major achievement not altogether incomparable with the miracle of wartime production.

Inflationary Potentialities of Debt Already Created

I now come to consider what inflationary potentialities, if any, are present in the existence of a public debt once it has been created. Let us assume that the war is over and that fresh public borrowings have ceased. What now of the effect of existing debt? Is its effect inflationary, deflationary, or neutral?

Let us assume that the government budget is balanced and that the debt remains constant at a fixed level. If some individuals cash in their bonds, the Treasury places new issues either with the public who wish to buy more bonds out of current savings or with the commercial banks.

Let us assume that new issues, equivalent to those cashed in, are placed with the public who wish to invest current savings. What are the inflationary or deflationary potentialities inherent in this situation? Well, that all depends. We need to know, in addition to the conditions already enumerated, what the balance is between private savings and private investment. We assume here no net borrowing by the government—the new issues merely replace the bonds cashed in. Let us assume, also, a balance between net saving and net private investment in new plant, equipment, housing, and other forms of capital formation. This means that total saving is adequate to cover private investment and also adequate to cover the dis-saving of those who cash in their bonds. Under these circumstances, the new government issues which must be placed to offset the bonds that are cashed, do not compete with private investment for loanable funds. No inflationary potentialities are present. If, on the other hand, current saving is not adequate to cover both private net investment and the new government bonds issued to replace those cashed in, inflationary potentialities *will* be present.

In the event that private investment is at a level inadequate to absorb net private saving, deflationary tendencies will be present in the economy when the government's new issues just balance the old bonds cashed in. To offset the excess of net private saving over private investment, and to prevent this deflationary tendency, the government would have to engage in loan expenditures thereby adding to the volume of public debt.

It follows from the analysis which I have just made that the maintenance of a public debt already created in and of itself has neither inflationary nor deflationary potentialities. If private investment exceeds net private saving, inflationary tendencies will be present in the economy when the level of the public debt is maintained. This inflationary tendency could be offset by a budgetary surplus and the retirement of public debt. But, of course, if there were no public debt, the inflationary tendency could equally be offset by a budgetary surplus—in this case the Treasury holding the surplus in idle balances.

We have now reached a point in our analysis, however, which compels us to examine the difference between a budgetary surplus held in idle balances and a budgetary surplus used to retire debt. The former automatically effectively offsets any inflationary tendencies inherent in an excess of private investment over net private saving. The latter may or may not do so. If the debt is retired, the first question is: What kinds of taxes are employed? Some are more contractionist than others. The second question is: Who are the bondholders that are relinquishing the bonds for cash? If it is the banks, the retirement of the debt will have substantially the same contractionist effect as the holding of the Treasury surplus in idle balances. True, the liabilities and assets of the commercial banks being reduced through the debt retirement process, excess reserves would be somewhat higher, but this situation by itself alone is not likely to lead to an offsetting increase in private expenditures.

If the sellers of bonds should use the cash to buy stock market securities, some inflationary development in stock prices might occur which, however, again would not of itself result necessarily in any increase in expenditures affecting the cost of living. If the bonds are cashed in by persons who wish to use the proceeds to buy housing or durable consumers' goods, or to increase their expenditures generally, the effect would be expansionist in the market for goods. But this again would not necessarily involve any price inflation or any increase in the cost of living if unused resources are available to match the increased effective demand with more goods and services. The conclusion evidently is that the retirement of debt may have inflationary potentialities in certain circumstances, whereas the salting away of a budgetary surplus in idle balances clearly permits the contractionist effect of a budgetary surplus to have its full effect in offsetting the assumed excess of net investment over net saving.

Magnitude of Debt

Thus far in the analysis, it makes no difference whether the public debt is large or small. But now at last we must face the problem of size. Does the presence of a *large* public debt inherently have inflationary or deflationary potentialities as compared with the existence of a relatively small public debt? So far we have considered only the effect of marginal increases or decreases in the volume of debt but not the magnitude of the debt itself.

The inflationary or deflationary potentialities of the magnitude of the debt itself relate fundamentally to the effect of a given debt volume upon income distribution. The existence of a large public debt may profoundly affect income distribution, depending fundamentally upon who holds the bonds and who pays the taxes required to service the bonds. If the distribution of income is more highly concentrated as a result of the existence of a large public debt, on balance the tendency will be for such a society to save more and thereby intensify the savings-investment problem. If, however, there is a wide mass distribution of bonds, coupled with a steeply progressive tax structure, the effect may be a more equal distribution of income.

Impact of Large Public Debt Upon Investment

The effect of a large public debt must also be measured in terms of its impact on investment. The tax structure will obviously be affected by the size of the public debt. If the net effect of the distribution of bond holdings and the distribution of taxes is such as to increase consumption, may it not, on the other side, correspondingly or even more reduce investment and thus act in a deflationary manner? This may indeed be so; but not necessarily. It depends upon whether a tax structure can be devised that does not impinge upon the inducement to invest or at least not sufficiently to offset any possible favorable effect upon consumption. Here we encounter the question: If one goes light on consumption taxes in order to affect favorably income distribution and stimulate consumption, where then shall one tax? Obviously the remaining main fields are corporate income taxation and personal income taxation. It is my belief that a tax structure that goes light on corporate income taxation and relies more heavily upon a progressive personal income tax is more favorable for investment than one which taxes corporations heavily and personal incomes lightly.

With respect to both forms of taxes, it may be pointed out that generous loss carry-back and loss carry-forward minimize very much any restraining effect which taxation may have upon the inducement to invest. Indeed, the thesis has been advanced—which needs thorough examination—that if the loss carry-back and loss carry-forward principle is developed to the limit so that the Treasury shares in losses on the same basis as it shares in profits, the inducement to invest and to assume risk is not unfavorably affected at all. We are currently witnessing the undoubted fact that an enormous amount of venturesome experimentation in the development of new processes and new products is going on, stimulated by the excess profits tax. It would be going too far to assume, as is usually done, that taxes necessarily must adversely affect investment. In addition to a greater or a less sharing on the part of the Treasury in losses as well as profits, there are also the vast possibilities inherent in tax incentive devices. These are matters that must be much more adequately explored than they have hitherto been before any clear judgment can be reached on a very intricate and complex problem.

Effect of Debt Upon Savings

In so far as the taxes needed to service the public debt do have an adverse effect on investment, the potentialities of a public debt are deflationary, not inflationary.

Apart from the effect on income distribution, there is the further question as to how the mere fact of large bond holdings may affect the disposition to spend and to save. If people hold a considerable amount of bonds, will they tend to spend more out of current income than would be the case if they held no bonds? I have heard fairly convincing arguments on both sides of this question. I do not think the answer is at all clear. There is a good deal of experience to the effect that a nest egg of savings stimulates an appetite for more savings. The effect will vary widely with different individuals. What I think is clear, however, is that in the case of distress and prolonged unemployment, widespread ownership of bonds will act as a cushion enabling people to maintain their standard of living or at least to reduce it less than would be necessary if they did not have this nest egg of savings to fall back upon. From this standpoint, the presence of a large public debt acts as a counter factor against severe depression. The public debt has, therefore, under these circumstances counter-deflationary potentialities.

Effect of Service Charges Upon Credit of Government

What of the argument that the service charges may become so heavy as to threaten the credit of the government? May not inflationary potentialities lurk here?

This line of reasoning is frequently buttressed by historical illustrations drawn from earlier centuries and often from undeveloped and primitive economies. The taxable capacities of primitive and poor countries is very low. Savings institutions are lacking. Loanable funds are available in very limited quantity. There is no well-developed money and capital market. Banking facilities are inadequate and there is no powerful central bank to stabilize the market for high-grade securities.

The inflationary experiences of primitive and poor countries with weak taxing powers and inadequate savings and banking facilities, are, it should be stressed, not at all pertinent to the public debt problems of countries like the United States, Canada, or Great Britain. In all these countries the taxable capacity is enormous, the volume of savings very great, and the banking institutions, including powerful central banks, are highly developed. The credit of modern governments in advanced countries surpasses by far that of any institution, public or private, in all history.

But we must defend that credit. Government credit is the foundation of our whole financial structure. In the great depression it was government credit that came to the rescue of bankrupt railroads, bankrupt banks, bankrupt home owners, and bankrupt land owners. Government credit underlies the security of our savings institutions, our insurance companies, our commercial banks, and our entire credit system.

There are currently dangerous attacks being made upon the credit of the federal government. Resolutions have passed a number of state legislatures proposing a constitutional amendment to limit the taxing powers of the federal government. Even before the Constitution was adopted, Alexander Hamilton, in his federalist papers, argued that any limitation on the taxing power of the federal government would be a grave mistake. If, as is now suggested, we should, by constitutional amendment, deprive Congress of the power to impose income tax rates in excess of 25 per cent, will not others propose an amendment to raise exemptions to $3,500 and to limit the rate on the lower incomes? Proposals have also been made to limit the borrowing power of the federal government. Such proposals should be vigorously resisted by all who have any regard for the integrity and security of our financial institutions. If our social order is to survive we must maintain the credit of the government, the purchasing power of our money and the value of government bonds.

It is not without significance that a cardinal principle of English fiscal policy, as Sir James Steuart remarked as far back as 1767, was to maintain the credit rating of government bonds. The public debt rose in England at a prodigious rate for 150 years from the time of the founding of the Bank of England to the end of the Napoleonic wars. And this debt was not retired. Instead, policy was directed toward maintaining the value of the bonds already outstanding. It may be truly said that this policy provided a rock bottom foundation for the security and integrity of public and private finance.

With the vast volume of savings which our society generates at even moderate employment levels, with our well-developed savings and banking institutions, our Federal Reserve System, and the taxable capacity inherent in a society capable of producing a 150 billion dollar national income, we need have no fears about any inflationary potentialities springing from a breakdown of the federal credit. But we could dangerously weaken that credit if we impose serious limitations upon the taxing and borrowing powers of the federal government.

CHAPTER VI

INFLATIONARY POTENTIALITIES OF THE PUBLIC DEBT

JAMES F. HUGHES

Smith, Barney & Company

APPROACHING this problem from the viewpoint of economic theory, I am forced to concede that skillful economic management of fiscal policies can neutralize both the inflationary and deflationary potentialities of the public debt. Approaching the problem from a long-range historical viewpoint, however, I am fearful that unexpected and possibly disastrous results ultimately will develop from the use of public debt as a dynamic factor in creating bank deposit purchasing power.

Not enough publicity has been given the fact that since 1933 public debt has become the controlling factor in continuing the progressive expansion of bank credit that has been under way in this country for the past hundred years. The problem of skillful economic management of the public debt has thus been tremendously complicated by using more than 50 billion dollars of federal debt since 1933 to manufacture bank credit purchasing power. Spectacular gyrations in the expansion and contraction of bank credit during the past thirty years have contributed materially to the acceleration of economic trends and I am afraid that as a nation we are well along in another dazzling experiment with bank credit that will have the conventional unexpected ending in some kind of catastrophe.

Transition from Private Credit to Public Debt

I want to make it perfectly clear that my personal feeling is strongly against the use of public debt as the controlling financial factor in our economic life. As an observer of actual developments, however, I cannot afford to cater to personal prejudices. As a spectator on the sidelines I must admit that for the past fifteen years the use of public debt has been the controlling financial factor in our economy. Furthermore, I can see no justification for projecting any change in the trend toward primary dependence on public debt in peace as well as war.

This conclusion is based on the ease with which public debt has been able to create bank credit purchasing power during the past ten years. From June, 1933, to June, 1943, the direct and guaranteed debt of the federal government increased $118 billion. Of this increase all private banks in the United States absorbed $50 billion, or 42 per cent. The Federal Reserve Banks increased their holdings by $4.7 billion and government agencies and trust funds by $10.5 billion. All the other investors in the nation bought $53 billion of Treasury securities, or 45 per cent of the increase in the federal debt.

From a bank credit viewpoint the interesting item in these statistics is the increase of $50 billion in private bank holdings of U. S. Treasury securities. Largely as a result of this absorption of public debt, the deposits of the commercial banks increased $58 billion, from $27 billion in 1933 to $85 billion in 1943. Of this increase in deposits $50 billion of painlessly created bank deposit purchasing power may be credited to the fiscal operations of the federal government. Acceleration in the use of bank credit purchasing power since the war is reflected in the fact that of the $50 billion involved, $11 billion was created in the six years 1933 to 1939 and $39 billion in the following four years.

Prior to 1930 the dynamic factor in creating bank deposit purchasing power was the loan function of the banks. During the twenty years preceding 1930 there was an increase of $24 billion in the loans of commercial banks. Accompanying this expansion of the loan account the banks increased their investment holdings by $11 billion. This $35 billion increase in bank assets produced an expansion of $32 billion in deposits, from $12 billion in 1910 to $44 billion in 1930.

But this spectacular performance represented the climax in bank credit expansion under private auspices. From 1930 to June, 1933, there was a liquidation of $18 billion in bank loans with the investment account showing no change for these three years. At this juncture public debt assumed control of bank credit expansion and in ten years created $50 billion of deposit purchasing power, or $18 billion more than World War I and the New Era boom were able to manufacture over a span of twenty years. On net balance for the ten-year period following June, 1933, private enterprise showed no increase in bank borrowing. Total loans for all the banks in June, 1943, amounted to $22.2 billion as compared with $22.3 in 1933.

Continuance of Public Debt as Controlling Factor

The foregoing sums up the statistical record of the transition from private credit to public debt as the dynamic force in the creation of bank deposit purchasing power. Following are some of the reasons why it seems logical to expect public debt to continue as the controlling factor in bank credit expansion:

1. The ease with which wholesale credit expansion is accomplished by one agency as compared with the tremendous labor involved in

credit expansion on a relatively retail basis by hundreds of thousands of private borrowers.

2. The great advantage of having only one form of collateral—U. S. Treasury securities—as the basis for bank credit expansion. The price structure of this collateral is relatively docile and is much more easily controlled than the commodity price structure of 1920 or the stock price structure of 1929.

3. The reformation of the securities markets and the wealth and income sharing tax policies of the past ten years have eliminated the stock market as a dynamic factor in bank credit expansion.

4. With our national economy habituated over the past hundred years to the approximate doubling of bank credit purchasing power each decade, the only method left that can successfully handle the problem is the continued generous use of public debt.

Of these four reasons only the last one requires any detailed elaboration. The following table shows the actual deposits of all commercial banks in the United States for each ten-year period since 1840 compared with the hypothetical volume of deposits if they had exactly doubled during each decade:

DEPOSITS OF ALL COMMERCIAL BANKS LESS INTER-BANK DEPOSITS

(In Billions)

Year (June 30)	Actual Amount	Hypothetical Decade Doubling
1840	$ .076	$ .076
1850	.110	.152
1860	.254	.304
1870	.598	.608
1880	1.1	1.2
1890	2.7	2.4
1900	5.1	4.9
1910	11.6	9.7
1920	32.1	19.5
1930	44.0	39.0
1940	49.0	78.0
1943	85.2	101.4
1943 (Dec. 31 est.)	100 to 105	105.3
1950	?	156.0
1960	?	312.0

This table reveals the progressive increase in the use of bank credit since 1840. Decades in which outstanding bank deposits failed to double, as in the seventies and nineties, were followed by decades in which they more than doubled. It is interesting to note that in the decade of World War I, when deposits nearly tripled, some of the benefits of this expansion were carried over into the twenties, and while the net expansion from 1920 to 1930 was only $12 billion this was enough to maintain the ten-year doubling rate for the 1910-1930 period.

The economic disasters of the thirties are reflected in the net increase in deposits of only $5 billion from the $44 billion level of 1930. The jump to $85 billion for June, 1943, while somewhat belated, is nevertheless maintaining the progressive rate of bank credit expansion which according to the hundred-year record has been essential to keep our economy operating at a satisfactory level of general business activity and employment. It is of interest to note that the estimate of commercial bank deposits as of the end of 1943 is in close alignment with the interpolated hypothetical deposits for that year.

This record of progressive expansion of bank credit purchasing power does not mean that credit and monetary factors are the primary cause of business cycle fluctuations. The fundamental causes of major cycles are undoubtedly associated with important technological changes, with great wars, with the exploration, settling and development of new territories and with relatively long waves of new construction. These forces may be accepted as the primary factors in major cycles but in actual practice they become effective through the medium of capital investment and their influence on business fluctuations is accelerated or retarded for significant periods of time by important changes in the rate of expansion or contraction of bank credit.

Business Depressions Foreshadowed by Bank Credit Developments

Without going into the substantiating details I know I am justified in saying that all major business depressions since the Civil War have been foreshadowed by developments in the bank credit field, that the protracted depressions have been accompanied by relatively important liquidation and subsequent stagnation in bank credit, and that the successive peaks reached in the rate of industrial activity have all been associated with new peaks in the use of bank credit. Despite this record I have always acknowledged the distinctly secondary role of credit and monetary factors.

Recently, however, I have been considering the possibility that the progressive increase in the rate of bank credit purchasing power may have reached a stage in which even as a secondary factor its importance in cyclical fluctuations may be much greater than generally conceded. It is obvious that the rate of bank credit expansion has far exceeded the rate of increase in industrial production and national income. National income per capita in 1860 has been estimated at $121. Per capita bank deposits in 1860 were only $8.06. By 1910 per capita income had increased to $353 and bank deposits to $126. Ten years later the income level was $662 and bank deposits $301. In 1943 income per capita reached $1,052 and deposits $631. The ratio of per capita income to deposits for 1860, 1910, 1920 and 1943 was 15.0, 2.8, 2.2 and 1.7 respectively.

The evidence shows increases in national income have been accompanied by a much more rapid increase in the rate of expansion of bank credit purchasing power. Certainly the record of spectacular gyrations in bank credit since 1910, particularly in the twenties and early thirties, seems to support the viewpoint that the accelerating and retarding influence of this secondary factor has been relatively much more powerful than it was in earlier decades.

Between 1910 and 1920 more than $20 billion of bank deposits were created. From the peak, late in 1920, to the low point in 1921 about $4 billion of deposits were liquidated. From this low there was an expansion of $16 billion to 1930, followed by the liquidation of $17 billion in the next three years. The use of U. S. Treasury securities as collateral for bank credit expansion has been the controlling factor in the creation of $73 billion of bank deposits since 1933.

These fantastic gyrations in relatively short periods of time have undoubtedly greatly accelerated some of the economic trends set in motion by such primary factors as wars, technological changes, and construction cycles. The use of public debt in the manufacture of bank credit purchasing power provides an opportunity to make bank credit expansion a primary factor in the business cycle with technological changes and construction cycles artificially forced by lavish government spending.

Reason for Expecting Catastrophe

Now that public debt has been elected by default to this dubious honor, we come to the important question, "Will public debt succeed in stabilizing economic fluctuations without ultimately producing disastrous inflationary results?" As I have already indicated, my personal prejudice is that ultimately continued expansion of the public debt to create bank deposit purchasing power will result in some kind of catastrophe.

I think I can most easily sum up my reason for expecting ultimate catastrophe in the statement that the public debt is now in politics. This means that the public debt is going to get political rather than economic handling. I am willing to concede that skillful, prudent management of fiscal policy, wisely timing government expenditures, expansion and contraction of bank debt, and changes in the incidence of taxation to meet changing conditions, might well produce reasonably full utilization of our material and human resources over a long period of time. Unfortunately, however, I doubt whether political pressure will permit skillful, prudent management of fiscal policy.

In using the phrase "political pressure" I do not mean anything crude or sinister. The adoption of conscious management of anything as vast and complex as the economic activities of this country will automatically create perfectly normal human and social pressures that will seriously interfere with the unemotional economic processes required for skillful, prudent management of fiscal policy.

On the basis of past history I am positive that perfectly normal human political pressure will constantly be working for an ever-increasing, ascending spiral of business prosperity, which means an ever-increasing, ascending spiral of bank deposits. This conclusion is thoroughly justified by our experience with the management of bank credit during the past century.

Everything has been relatively satisfactory while we were manufacturing and using bank credit purchasing power. Conditions have been far from satisfactory during those periods when we have had to substract from current purchasing power to pay off previously created purchasing power.

Future Problems

The problem for the future is how to avoid periodic phases of bank credit liquidation or even wide fluctuations in the rate of bank credit expansion. This is too intricate a problem for successful political management. If it were even generally realized that bank credit, through the medium of the public debt, is one of our most critical domestic political problems, there might be some chance of success in managing it. Unfortunately, the problem of bank credit is something that the vast majority of people doesn't know exists and that many of the small minority conscious of it, believe to be a relatively minor secondary result of far more important primary economic forces.

Under these conditions I have very little faith in the perpetual stabilization of economic trends by the use of public debt in the creation of bank credit purchasing power. The lesson of previous history is that the progressively increased use of bank credit has produced progressively wilder gyrations in economic trends.

The creation of more than fifty billion dollars of bank deposit purchasing power in the past four years will ultimately produce serious problems for solution. In all probability the first of these problems will be how to sustain in peacetime the level of industrial activity, employment, and national income of the past few years without the assistance of continued manufacture of bank deposit purchasing power at the wartime rate. On the basis of trends during the past decade any early postwar deflationary threat will in all likelihood be met by further resort to public debt for bank credit expansion. A normal industrial recovery spiral based on the deferred demand of the war period should contribute to bank credit expansion for several years.

Beyond this point, however, will be the time to watch for the unexpected results from our wholesale use of public debt in the manufacture of bank deposit purchasing power. The choice will then be between running the risk of more important deflationary trends or attempting artificial forcing of industrial activity and employment. I think the latter policy will prevail and in this event we shall in all probability witness the ultimate inflationary potentialities of the public debt.

PART THREE

FISCAL DEVICES FOR CURBING INFLATION

CHAPTER VII

A FEDERAL RETAIL SALES TAX AS A FISCAL DEVICE FOR CURBING INFLATION IN WARTIME[1]

MARIUS FARIOLETTI

Division of Tax Research, Treasury Department

IN DISCUSSING the much debated subject of the sales tax as a fiscal device for curbing inflation in wartime, the sales tax, like other tax measures, should be viewed as supplementary to existing nonfiscal inflation controls and not as an alternative to such controls. As a second line of defense, the general sales tax should bolster, and not hinder, the first line of defense, namely, price and wage controls.

Even "taxes for revenue" do not operate in a vacuum and it is necessary to lift up the hood over the inflation control machinery to see whether the sales tax gears will mesh, or simply mash. Distasteful as it may be to those who like clean-cut answers, we must admit that the sales tax has both deflationary and inflationary effects. What must be discovered, and weighed in the balance, are the weights of these opposing effects. The problem is easy conceptually, but as a matter for practical determination it is very difficult.

Before proceeding to the more specific consideration of the anti-inflationary and inflationary aspects of a general sales

[1] For a more complete discussion of the sales tax as a wartime revenue measure, see U. S. Treasury Department, "Considerations Respecting a Federal Retail Sales Tax," reprinted in Hearings before Committee on Ways and Means on *Revenue Revision of 1943*, pp. 1095-1272.

tax, let us not forget the oft-forgotten step of specifying the kind of sales tax to be analyzed. This issue should not be skipped over too hurriedly, for the kind of sales tax selected plays a part in determining its effectiveness as an anti-inflationary device.

Let us rule out the multiple-stage or "turnover" type of sales tax, since it is clearly incompatible with existing price controls. Of the so-called single-stage taxes, the retail sales tax is preferable to either the manufacturers' or wholesale taxes. The retail tax would entail the least interference with price controls and the least amount of pyramiding. It is most adaptable to the inclusion of services, agricultural products, and secondhand goods, and would return the largest revenue per unit of tax rate. The latter point is important because, among other things, high tax rates increase administrative difficulties.

The retail tax would appear to be more difficult to administer, not only because of the larger number of taxpayers involved but also because relatively more of them would have inadequate records. But, here too, there are countervailing considerations such as the almost complete avoidance of valuation problems. On balance, the retail sales tax would fit the wartime needs better than either of the other two single-stage taxes.[2]

Now that we have selected the retail sales tax for analysis, what shape shall it take?[3] If the tax is to have important anti-inflationary effects, it must make a sizable dent in the so-called gross inflationary gap of about $40 billion. Let us assume that a rate of about 10 per cent is called for even though

---

[2] *Ibid.*, "Factors Affecting the Choice of a Retail Sales Tax in Preference to the Other Types of Sales Taxes," pp. 1115-23.

[3] For a discussion of "Factors Affecting the Structure of a Federal Retail Sales Tax Under Wartime Conditions," see *ibid.*, pp. 1124-60.

such a high rate may be above the political maximum. Let us assume further, that the tax applies to the widest base consistent with administrative practicability and with price controls, even though this would mean taxing food, clothing, and medicine. Such a tax might apply to all retail sales of tangible personal property except sales of certain "cost goods" such as fuel, industrial, agricultural and commercial machinery, and feed, seed, and fertilizer. In addition, the tax might apply to certain services usually rendered on a commercial basis by established business enterprises, including repair, fabrication and rental of taxable articles, laundry and dry cleaning, and services of barber shops and beauty parlors.

At 10 per cent, such a tax would yield about $6 billion.[4] This would not zip the gap, and the estimated budgetary deficit would still be over $50 billion.[5] But $6 billion of additional tax revenue is of a size to help dampen the inflationary spending power. We should not, however, set up the problem as a choice between a 10 per cent sales tax and serious additional price increases. I do not believe we can work the sales tax issue down to the point where taxpayers must choose either a certain but limited increase in the cost of living of, say, 10 per cent as a consequence of a general sales tax, or an uncertain but unlimited increase in the absence of the sales tax.

Deflationary Side of the Sales Tax

The deflationary side of the retail sales tax may be explained by describing the withdrawal of spending power from buyers and their responsiveness to tax-induced price increases.

---

4 *Ibid.*, p. 1151.

5 *The Budget of the United States Government for the Fiscal Year Ending June 30, 1945*, p. xxi.

Assuming that sellers would shift the tax forward to buyers, there would be a tendency, in the first instance, for the gross inflationary gap to decrease by the amount of tax collected. If buyers did not go into debt or draw down their accumulated savings in the attempt to maintain their pre-tax level of physical purchases, their current spending power would be decreased by the amount of the tax. That is, if the government breaks into the wartime price-income cycle by erecting a sales tax diversionary canal, the income flow is tapped for its account. Such tax-induced price increases mean, in the first instance, higher prices for things civilians buy, but not increases in their incomes. The $6 billion tax canal flows into the Treasury and out again into a $100 billion expenditure stream[6] that flows back into the income river. This tax diversionary process is continuous and reduces the size of the gross gap, other things remaining equal.

The sales tax would also be deflationary to the extent that it influenced consumers to reduce their spending in response to the tax-induced price increases. Some consumers might prefer to forego present purchases and to save more as a result of the tax. We may observe in passing, that many consumers would avoid significant amounts of sales tax, in the first year, by practicing the art of forward buying. There is likely to be such a long time between proposal, acceptance and effective date of a new tax of this kind, that there would be ample opportunity for those with spending power to anticipate their future needs. Forward buying cannot be classed as deflationary! After the tax is enacted, some consumers might shift their purchases from taxable to non-taxable goods and services. This type of adjustment would not necessarily be deflationary.

Sales-tax-induced decreases in propensities to consume are

---

[6] *Ibid.*, p. xvii.

difficult to evaluate and, certainly, cannot be measured by referring to the revenue yield. The more people forego spending, the smaller the yield. However, during a period of general shortages in the supplies of civilian goods and substantial excess spending power, too much emphasis probably should not be placed on this deflationary aspect of the sales tax.

If excess spending power were distributed among consumers at a constant percentage of their taxable expenditures, the sales tax might be bored to rifle precision. But excess spending power has no tendency to distribute itself in such a way as to transform the mantelpiece blunderbuss into a facsimile of the Garand rifle. Since excess spending power is not evenly distributed among income brackets or within any income bracket,[7] a sales tax would not siphon off enough excess spending power from some consumers and would take more than enough from others. The latter group of consumers would have to decrease either their consumption or savings. To the extent that savings were decreased, the immediate anti-inflationary effects of the tax would be reduced. I do not know how much of the estimated $6 billion sales tax yield would represent decreases in savings, but I believe it would be significant.

To the extent that price controls and rationing are effective, excess spending power is transformed into savings. A considerable portion of the 1943 excess spending power, for example, wound up as liquid savings. Spendable consumer income increased from $109 billion in 1942 to $124 billion in 1943. Consumer expenditures increased from $84 billion to $91 billion, and perhaps $5 billion of this $7 billion increase is

7 U. S. Treasury Department, "The Need for More Taxes—Appendix A," reprinted in Hearings before Committee on Ways and Means on *Revenue Revision of 1943*, pp. 30-31.

attributable to price increases.[8] Liquid savings of consumers increased from $25 billion to $33 billion.[9]

The important point is that the indicated $38 billion gross gap was resolved into about $33 billion of liquid savings and about $5 billion of price increases. The important question is whether consumer expenditures (including sales tax) would have been closer to $97 billion or $92 billion, if a $6 billion retail sales tax had been in effect in 1943. My opinion is that expenditures would have been closer to $97 billion.

If this is true, a substantial portion of the $6 billion sales tax yield would have been extracted from liquid savings, and this portion of the yield would not have been deflationary in the short run. Of course, to the extent that these savings are not effectively immobilized they constitute an inflationary threat. If people were to lose confidence in the continuing effectiveness of price controls, substantial amounts of liquid resources might pour into the markets with disastrous price-increasing effects. But the exceptionally high savings of individuals in the past two years also indicate an appreciation of the great problems to be faced in the postwar period. The problems of reconversion, postwar income decreases, and unemployment loom large and dark. People want to be in the best financial position possible to meet the great uncertainties, for the problems of the last depression are still clearly remembered. Uncertainty breeds a high liquidity preference and, if there is one thing the war has given us in excess

---

8 Estimate based upon the price changes reported in the Bureau of Labor Statistics cost-of-living index.

9 Estimates of the Department of Commerce and the Treasury Department. The Commerce estimates of consumer expenditures and net savings of individuals have been adjusted slightly to classify consumer expenditures on certain capital goods with spendings rather than savings. For unadjusted estimates see "The American Economy in 1943," *Survey of Current Business,* January, 1944, p. 17.

of demand, it is uncertainty of postwar economic stability.

It is important to understand that not all of the sales tax dollars would represent dollars that would have been spent. A significant portion would represent dollars that would have been saved. A clearer understanding of these mechanics, followed by more research in the income-expenditure distribution field, would tend to resolve some of the differences among proponents and opponents of sales versus net income taxes. Now that the income tax is collected currently, it is very doubtful whether the sales tax is mechanically superior to the income tax as a deflationary fiscal device, except in so far as the sales tax reaches those below the agreed-upon income tax exemption levels.

Reductions in consumption consequent to a retail sales tax would be most effective in the lowest income brackets, where consumers spend all or more than they receive on the bare necessities of life. In the middle income brackets, consumption would also be reduced but by significantly smaller amounts than indicated by the dollar tax payments. These people would tend to draw down their past or current savings. Among the higher income consumers, reductions in consumption would be negligible, for the tax would probably be paid almost entirely from income that would have been saved.

Although the sales tax would tend to reduce somewhat the money volume of consumer spending (exclusive of tax) during wartime years like 1942, 1943, and perhaps 1944, there probably would be no noticeable decrease in the aggregate physical quantity of goods and services consumed. When consumer demand exceeds the available supplies by amounts so considerable that general price controls and rationing are necessary, tax-induced decreases in consumption by some consumers would probably be almost entirely offset by increases in consumption by other consumers more fortunately situated. In the case of rationed goods, offsetting increases in consumption might be limited somewhat. If the decrease in rationed commodities were significant, however, the ration values probably would be changed to clear the markets of the allocated civilian supplies.

The Question of the Final Incidence of a Sales Tax

So far we have been discussing the deflationary aspects of the sales tax with the help of two very convenient assumptions: first, that sellers would pass on the full amount of the sales tax to consumers and, second, that consumers could not pass the tax on.

We have already indicated that the portion of the tax applying to sales to individual consumers generally could be expected to be passed on to them. The shifting of the tax applying to sales to industrial and commercial users will be discussed later. The very great increases in the liquid savings of individuals in 1942 and 1943 indicate that the general price controls have been quite effective in reducing the amount consumers have had to spend for the available supplies of goods and services.[10] It now appears that in 1944 the wartime peak of disposable consumer income will be reached, and that civilian production may not be expanded significantly. Further important increases in the amount of liquid savings of individuals are likely under existing price controls. These general conditions are very favorable for shifting the tax to consumers. No doubt, there would be a number of commodities where retailers could not add the entire 10 per cent tax without reducing sales significantly. But, in general,

[10] *Ibid.* See also the Office of Price Administration charts portraying effects of price controls on the cost of living, OPA-3849, released January 31, 1944.

prices seem to be ceiled sufficiently below the demand level to permit adding the tax without reducing total dollar sales (exclusive of tax) to any appreciable extent.

Perhaps the most important basis for the widely held opinion that a sales tax would be deflationary is the general belief that once the tax was passed on to consumers it would rest there.[11] This belief is the roughest sort of first approximation and is not even consistent with the theory of perfect competition which is the apparent starting point for the usual analyses of sales tax shifting and incidence. Under the classical theory of distribution, the prices of the factors of production must all be reduced as a result of a general sales tax, else there would be disequilibrium and unemployment, which is quite inconsistent with long-run equilibrium economies.[12]

It is of paramount importance that tax economists devote as much attention to the conditions under which sales taxes may be shifted by consumers as they have to the shifting of the taxes by sellers. Consumers are also producers. Interest and wage rates are also prices, and are just as much a part of the problem of sales tax incidence as are the prices of the commodities taxed.

During the past two years, resources of almost all types have been scarce in the sense that market demand exceeded supply at the existing prices. Direct government controls, taxes, and the high level of individual savings have been effective in keeping price increases in hand. From August, 1939, to December, 1943, the BLS cost-of-living index in-

[11] Wehrwein, Carl F., "Taxes and The Consumer," *The American Economic Review,* XXVIII (March, 1938), 92.

[12] Brown, H. G., "The Incidence of a General Output or a General Sales Tax," *Journal of Political Economy,* XLVII (April, 1939) 257; and "The Incidence of a General Output or a General Sales Tax: A Correction," XLVII (June, 1939) 418. See also Due, J. F., *The Theory of Incidence of Sales Taxation,* King's Crown Press, New York, 1942, pp. 32, 114, 148, 164-65.

creased about 26 per cent. From December, 1942, to December, 1943, however, the index increased only a little more than 3 per cent. The threat of inflation continues to be a big problem; but the Department of Commerce, in its review of "The American Economy in 1943" recently stated,

> . . . it seemed possible that if the "hold the line" policy on prices and wage rates could be substantially maintained for 6 months or so, that even this problem would have successfully withstood its most critical period.[13]

Many social and economic pressures and administrative difficulties are continually being encountered which threaten to disrupt the price stabilization machinery. How would a 10 per cent retail sales tax affect the "hold the line" policy? Would price ceilings be disturbed? What are the chances that some consumer groups would be able to offset the tax shifted to them by obtaining higher income? Would labor groups intensify their attempts to obtain wage-rate increases to offset the tax-induced increases in living costs? Would farm groups be able to offset the tax through farm price increases generated by the tax? These are some of the questions pertaining to the final incidence of the sales tax. They must be investigated before giving ready answers as to whether the sales tax is deflationary or inflationary.

Offsets to the Deflationary Side of the Sales Tax

The offsets to the deflationary side of the sales tax involve various attempts by buyers to shift the tax. These attempts would interfere with price and wage stabilization controls and seriously endanger the "hold the line" policy. In discussing these offsets, I want clearly to state that a price increase of 10 per cent due to the addition of a 10 per cent tax will not

---

13 *Op. cit.*, p. 2.

be considered inflationary. What will be considered inflationary are tax-induced price increases in excess of 10 per cent, and of a kind that do not appear to converge rapidly so that they would be the basis and cause of further price increases without materially increasing the elasticity of supply of goods and services available for civilians.

Some proponents of the sales tax have told me the tax is necessary to bolster the price stabilization program. When some of the inflationary pressures that would be generated by the tax are explained, more often than not, the answer has been that the government should "clamp down" and act vigorously to control these pressures. It should be recognized, however, that price and wage controls are not absolute. If they were, the inflationary pressures could be curbed without resort to taxes.

Effects on Business Costs

There appears to be a widely held opinion that a federal retail sales tax would apply only to sales to individual consumers for consumption purposes and not to sales of articles used by business concerns for production purposes. While this dichotomy of sales between consumers and business concerns is very useful for some purposes it is not practical for sales tax administration.

The concept which has been found to be most practicable for sales tax purposes defines retail sale as a sale of tangible personal property for use by the purchaser and not for resale. Sales for resale include sales of articles which become physical ingredients or component parts of other tangible personal property which is to be sold, and sales of articles to be sold in the same form as purchased. Thus, if an article is not purchased for resale as a physical ingredient, component part, or in the same form as purchased, it is a taxable retail sale, unless it is otherwise specifically excluded from the tax. This definition has no necessary relationship to the usual distinctions drawn between sales by retailers and sales by wholesalers or manufacturers. Many sales by manufacturers and wholesalers would be taxable. In contrast, some sales by concerns engaged primarily in the business of retailing would be sales for resale and, consequently, tax free.[14]

The administrative impracticability of confining the tax to sales to individual consumers is an important limitation on the deflationary aspects of the sales tax. The taxation of articles entering into the operating costs of business concerns whose prices are ceiled is incompatible with price ceiling controls. We have assumed that feed, seed, fertilizer, fuel and machinery could be excluded from the tax. I am not at all sure, however, that an administratively practicable solution could be found with respect to the machinery exclusion. Perhaps some practicable method could also be found to exclude from tax such capital items as sales of livestock for breeding purposes, work animals, dairy cows, and poultry for laying purposes.

Even if these exclusions were made, there would remain subject to tax many articles sold for use by business concerns. These would include certain durable equipment (other than machinery) such as tools, chairs, tables and desks; consumables (other than fuel) including lubricants, abrasives, and chemicals (other than those becoming physical ingredients); miscellaneous supplies, including cleaning materials, stationery, and light bulbs; and building materials and hardware. Estimated sales of such articles in either 1943 or 1944, for civilian production only, are over $6 billion, amounting to over $600 million of tax at a 10 per cent rate.[15]

---

[14] *Revenue Revision of 1943*, pp. 1125-37, 1210-13.

[15] *Ibid.*, pp. 176-77.

In many cases the tax-induced cost increases would be small enough to be absorbed by the buyers without resort to price ceiling increases, particularly since the business concerns could deduct the tax expense for income and excess profits tax purposes. In other cases, however, the resulting inequality of requiring the tax to be absorbed would create additional significant pressure for upward revision of price ceilings. The opening of price ceilings to permit forward shifting of sales tax would inevitably invite price increases in addition to the tax simply because there are many existing pressures against ceiling prices. Furthermore, because of the interdependency of prices, which economists take great pains to point out, increases in some ceiling prices would increase the pressure on other controlled prices. Six hundred million dollars is a lot of sales tax to ask business to absorb, even though the government would share part of the cost, particularly when the basic intent is to permit the tax to be shifted.

It should be clear that even under the retail form of sales tax, significant additional direct pressures against price ceilings would be introduced by the tax. These conflicts with price control should be reduced to a minimum, but it appears that administrative limits to tax enforcement would probably necessitate the taxation of an appreciable volume of "cost goods." In so far as ceilings would be revised upward, there would be the very real risk of price revisions in excess of the amount which could be attributable to the tax and also the risk that other price ceilings would be affected. The secondary spiralling effects would tend to converge rapidly if additional and firm governmental action was taken to limit or offset the tax-induced disturbance. But, we must remember that the tax is supposed to ease and not intensify the problems of direct control. In so far as the tax was absorbed by business, part of the tax would be shifted to the government and, consequently, the deflationary aspects would be decreased. There is also the question whether decreases in business net income would actually be deflationary.

Effects on Agricultural Prices

A federal retail sales tax would also conflict with the stabilization of agricultural prices. Because the tax would apply to the sale of items used in farm production as well as articles used in farm family living, it would increase the index of prices paid by farmers and, consequently, increase farm parity prices. In turn, increases in farm parity prices would tend to generate increases in price ceilings and support prices on farm products. Theoretically, these tax-induced price increases might be prevented by prohibiting the inclusion of the tax in the index of prices paid by farmers. I do not believe this possibility is at all realistic.[16] The intent of the index is to measure the actual prices paid by farmers; state sales taxes have always been taken into account in the index; and the existing pressures are operating in the direction of higher prices.

Some of the prices in the index of prices paid by farmers, such as feed, seed, and food prices, are also related to parity. For example, even though feeds were not taxed, the increase in the prices-paid index would raise the parity price of feeds. Therefore, in addition to the direct effects of the tax on prices of agricultural commodities and their products, there would tend to be a secondary set of price-increasing forces because farmers are not only producers but also consumers of farm products included in the index of prices they pay.

Forecasting the actual increases in farm prices and in the wholesale and retail prices of farm products related directly

---

16 *Revenue Revision of 1943*. Statement of Hon. Fred M. Vinson, Director of the Office of Economic Stabilization, p. 398.

and indirectly to parity prices is a very complicated matter, because of the different price situations respecting individual commodities and because of the time required for the tax influences to operate under the existing administrative and market processes. Generally speaking, the tax-induced changes are likely to fall into four groups: (1) Increases in the parity prices of products whose market and ceiling prices are at parity would tend to induce corresponding increases in market prices; (2) where support prices are related to parity prices, such as 85 per cent or 90 per cent of parity, products whose market prices are at the same level as their support prices would tend to increase in price as a result of higher support prices; (3) products whose market prices are above support levels but below ceiling prices would tend to increase in price only when the support prices were raised above the market prices;[17] (4) products whose market and ceiling prices are above parity would probably not increase in price, except when the new parity price exceeded the previous market price.[17] In the latter case, prices would tend to increase to the parity and ceiling level. Because farm products compete for scarce farm resources, tax-induced increases in the prices of some farm products might also require additional price adjustments for other farm products in order better to assure the attainment of production goals. It can be readily seen that the probable tax-induced price changes in the field of agriculture are quite complicated.

About a year ago an attempt was made to estimate the magnitude of these effects on food prices.[18] At that time it appeared that a 10 per cent sales tax with the exclusions already described, would have increased parity prices by 6 or

---

[17] In the case of some commodities falling into these two categories, it is possible, assuming the market is in equilibrium, that prices (net of tax) might be reduced as a consequence of the tax.

[18] "Considerations Respecting a Federal Retail Sales Tax," *op. cit.*, pp. 1193-98.

7 per cent. If the tax had become effective July 1, 1943, it appeared that the tax would have induced an average increase of 4 per cent in the index of prices received by farmers in 1944. It was estimated that retail food prices would have averaged 6 per cent higher in 1944. The addition of these indirect tax-induced price effects to a 10 per cent sales tax on foods resulted in an estimated increase of almost 17 per cent in the average retail food costs in 1944.

These estimates also indicated that, as a group, farmers would have paid more in sales tax in 1943 than the increase in incomes they would have received as a result of the tax-induced price increases. In 1944, however, after the administrative and market processes had had an opportunity to operate in response to the parity-price increases, farmers would have received more income as a result of price increases than they would have paid out for sales tax. Thus, the estimates indicated that the tax would have increased rather than decreased the spending power of farmers. It also appeared that processors and distributors of foodstuffs would have received some income increases as a result of the tax, thereby tending to reduce their net sales tax costs somewhat.

If it is assumed that the nonfarm consumer groups could not have obtained offsetting income increases, the tax would have been doubly effective in reducing their spending power. Under this assumption, the secondary spiralling effects of the tax-induced price increases would converge rapidly, since the problem is resolved by definition into the simple one of transfer payments within the nation.

This statement must be qualified, however, since the deflationary effects of the sales tax would be decreased to the extent that governmental expenditures for agricultural commodities and their products were increased. Moreover, the price-increasing effects of the tax on foods and livestock feeds are entirely inconsistent with the war subsidy payments program which was an important factor in preventing price rises during 1943.[19]

Effects on Wage Stabilization Program

So far we have assumed that although a retail sales tax would seriously interfere with the price stabilization program, the direct controls might be strong enough to keep the tax-induced price increases from generating unmanageable spiralling effects. We come now to the implications of the sales tax with respect to the wage stabilization program.

Under this program, demands for wage rate increases, based solely on cost-of-living increases, have been allowed up to 15 per cent of the average straight time hourly rates paid in January, 1941.[20] Because cost-of-living increases are substantially greater than the 15 per cent figure used in the Little Steel formula, the wage stabilization program is under continuous pressure.

The sales tax would intensify the already great pressures for wage rate increases by raising the cost of living. A 10 per cent retail sales tax would directly cause a 7 per cent increase in the Bureau of Labor Statistics cost-of-living index. The available estimates indicate the index might be increased an additional 3 per cent as a result of the indirect tax effects on food prices. Further increases in the cost of living would also occur to the extent that upward price-ceiling revisions were made as a result of taxing sales of articles entering into business costs.[21]

---

19 "The American Economy in 1943," *op. cit.*, p. 15.

20 See "Will the War Labor Board Hold the Line on Wages?", extemporaneous remarks by Wayne L. Morse, Public Representative, National War Labor Board, at the 21st Annual Agricultural Outlook Conference, Washington, D. C., October 18, 1943. Mimeograph, United States Department of Agriculture.

21 "Considerations Respecting a Federal Retail Sales Tax," *op. cit.*, p. 1198.

I do not believe that elimination of the tax from the cost-of-living index would lessen the demand for wage increases. The response of wage earners might be a further loss of confidence in the index.[22]

In addition to the cost-of-living approach to the effects of the sales tax on wage stabilization, some thought should be given to the psychological response of labor to this form of tax. Labor groups have consistently opposed a federal sales tax and feel it is a discriminatory tax aimed at low-income groups. Some of the labor representatives recently stated before the Ways and Means Committee that a sales tax would be equivalent to a national reduction in wages which would bear most heavily on low-income groups, and that organized labor would demand wage increases proportionate to the wage cut imposed by a federal sales tax.[23]

If a federal sales tax should raise parity prices and farm income, it is very doubtful whether the wage stabilization program could withstand wage-earner demands for similar offsets to the tax. Wage stabilization requires stabilization of prices entering into wage-earner living costs, and a 10 per cent sales tax would increase these prices significantly.

When the Director of the Office of Economic Stabilization appeared before the Ways and Means Committee last fall, he was asked specifically whether he could hold the line on the wage and salary front if a 10 per cent sales tax were imposed. He replied that he did not think it could be held.[24]

The danger that a sales tax would cause a significant breach

---

[22] See statement of A. F. Hinrichs, Acting Commissioner of Labor Statistics, respecting the preliminary draft of a recommended report submitted by the two labor members of the President's Committee on the Cost of Living: OWI-2905, January 30, 1944.

[23] *Revenue Revision of 1943, op. cit.,* statement of Philip Murray, President of the Congress of Industrial Organizations, p. 913; see also the following statements of other labor representatives, through p. 1006.

[24] *Ibid.,* p. 398.

in the wage stabilization program is an important consideration to be weighed against its deflationary aspects. We could better evaluate the risk that would be undertaken if it were feasible to estimate the amount of the wage increases that would result and the likely effects on prices, but this does not seem possible.

Subsequent Effects on Prices, Wages and Governmental Outlays

Increases in wages and prices as a result of the tax would form a basis for additional price and wage rises. The importance of these secondary spiralling effects would largely depend on the effectiveness of the direct price and wage controls. Some additional price and wage increases probably would be necessary but, how much, no one can say. Here we are again confronted with the incompatibility of the sales tax with existing direct controls. We start with the proposition that the tax would buttress direct controls and we find that we must depend on the direct controls to combat the inflationary tendencies of the tax.

There is one more point that should not be overlooked in evaluating the usefulness of the sales tax as a wartime deflationary device. Increases in wages and prices would also mean greater expenditures by the government. If we assume that the price and wage increases boosted both government expenditures and the sales tax base by equal amounts, then the additional expenditures would be ten times as large as the increase in the yield of a 10 per cent sales tax. In addition to the higher yield of the sales tax, there would also be some increases in the yields of other federal taxes. The difference between the higher governmental outlays attributable to the sales tax and the increased revenue yields must be deducted from the sales tax revenue. This deduction would decrease the deflationary effects of the sales tax resulting from the withdrawal of spending power.

Conclusions

In conclusion, it is evident that a federal retail sales tax would generate inflationary as well as deflationary pressures. Whether the tax would be deflationary or inflationary on balance is a very difficult question to answer. I believe it is conservative to state that even if the tax had a net deflationary effect, it is unlikely that it would contribute significantly to the wartime anti-inflation program. On the other hand, the inflationary aspects of the tax conflict so seriously with the existing price and wage stabilization machinery, that imposition of the tax would be a very risky undertaking.

In 1942, the Administrator of the Office of Price Administration stated "that general commodity taxation and price control do not go together."[25] In 1943, the Director of the Office of Economic Stabilization told the Ways and Means Committee that he did not think he could hold the line against inflation if a 10 per cent retail sales tax were levied.[26] The judgments of these officials respecting the incompatibility of the sales tax with wartime price and wage controls must be given very serious consideration.

For the various reasons brought out in this paper, it is my opinion that a federal retail sales tax cannot be recommended as a wartime anti-inflationary measure.

---

25 "Considerations Respecting a Federal Retail Sales Tax," *op. cit.*, p. 1235.

26 *Revenue Revision of 1943*, p. 398.

CHAPTER VIII

THE RETAIL SALES TAX

GODFREY N. NELSON

Secretary, The New York Times

IN THE TIME allotted to me I shall not attempt any historical treatment of the sales tax. Nor shall I discuss at length any form of sales tax other than that commonly referred to as the "retail sales tax," which I would briefly define as a tax upon the sale of personal property at retail.

RETAIL SALES TAX PREFERABLE

I chose the retail sales tax as my subject in preference to other forms of levies on sales because I believe this to be the most practicable and because the retail sales tax is particularly well adapted to the use of the federal government. Moreover, of the various taxes on sales, that on retail sales probably possesses the greatest potentiality for revenue. While the determination of the taxable base may not be quite as simple in practice as it appears in theory, the retail sales tax is comparatively free of the complexities and uneconomic qualities of the tax on turnover or the manufacturers' sales tax.

Inherent in the turnover tax is the unavoidable tendency toward pyramiding of the tax. The greater the number of processes through which a finished article passes in the course of manufacture, if performed by different taxpayers, the more often is the turnover tax applied. Whereas, if one taxpayer performed all the processes only one sales tax would be incurred. The duplication of the tax, therefore, would seem to condemn this kind of levy.

The manufacturers' sales tax, on the other hand, being imposed selectively on manufactured goods either as a finished product or as a finished unit of manufacture, can be made to avoid pyramiding. The difficulties in making such a tax operate without confusion and without pyramiding, however, could only be overcome by the exercise of great care and selectiveness in its administration. It has been said that the Canadian manufacturers' sales tax was in course of evolution for nearly a decade. Obviously such a tax would be unsuited for immediate use in an emergency.

Under ordinary peacetime conditions I would not favor a general sales tax at any but a nominal rate of one or two per cent because of its regressive character and its depressing effect upon trade. Unquestionably a retail sales tax deters the distribution of goods. In wartime, however, as a supplemental source of revenue, this form of taxation at a comparatively high rate is particularly suitable in that to the extent of its deterrence to consumption buying it tends to act as a preventive of inflation.

Nevertheless, the sales tax, imposed at low rates, can be regarded as an all-weather tax. Nearly a decade ago, when the sales tax movement was firmly taking root in the states, Professor Shoup described this tax as "a phenomenon of economic depressions," and he attributed its attractiveness to its apparent "painlessness."[1] It seemed "painless" primarily because it was passed on to the purchaser.

In 1934, sixteen states were employing sales taxes, most of them the retail sales tax. In spite of its shortcomings and

[1] *Proceedings of the National Tax Association, 1934*, p. 94.

despite the fact that some states have discarded the tax, its use has spread to 23 states and two municipalities. Although some states, including the state of New York, have abandoned the tax, it is noteworthy that a net growth in the number of states adopting the sales tax occurred in a period of depression.

Nevertheless, this expansion of its use has not convinced me that the sales tax at any but a low rate should be an acceptable form of tax in peacetime, and I would favor it still less in a period of depressed business activity. Yet, its attractiveness to legislators at a time when no needless drag upon business should have been permitted, indicates that this form of taxation possesses such a degree of merit as to have justified its continued use by many states.

If the tax is suitable to the state, it should be more suitable to the federal government. While the states employing the sales tax have largely overcome difficulties resulting from interstate delivery of goods, as by the enactment of "use" taxes, these administrative difficulties would not arise when employed by the federal government. There would be uniformity of geographic application, thus avoiding questions of interstate commerce.

Litigation is an important factor in the administration of tax laws. It is a matter of record that the sales tax has created less litigation in its use by the states than any federal tax in its use by the government. Unless we assume that a federal tax is resisted to a greater extent than a state tax, we may also assume that the federal government could administer a sales tax as economically and efficiently as any state.

Opposition to the Sales Tax

Opposition to the retail sales tax has been predicated on the claim that it is inflationary. It is argued that because the tax increases the cost of living to wage earners, the payment of the tax justifies demands for increased wages. The argument has been worn threadbare in behalf of labor groups in opposition to the sales tax. The answer seems to be that any tax, direct or indirect, deprives the taxpayer of otherwise spending the income absorbed by the tax. Therefore, generally speaking, opponents of the sales tax on this ground would seek obviously to avoid being taxed.

All shades of opinion on the sales tax will, I believe, recognize that there is a strong political undercurrent which is being assiduously directed against this tax. The arguments now used by the opposition are much the same as those heard shortly after the first World War, when it was sought to have the sales tax take the place of the excess profits tax. Present economic and governmental conditions, however, are entirely dissimilar.

Opponents of the tax would have us believe that the real objective of its proponents is to lighten the tax load of those in the upper brackets of the income tax; that they as a class are promoting a movement for the adoption of a sales tax for wholly selfish purposes. The fallacy of this reasoning is at once apparent by reference to the fact that total confiscation of net incomes of over $25,000 would yield but a fraction of the revenue that could be raised by a retail sales tax—probably less than 10 per cent.

On the other hand, while all income recipients should bear some share of the cost of the war, however slight, persons with only subsistence incomes should be allowed a sales tax exemption and there should be a slight increase in the present income tax exemptions. By what amounts the income tax exemptions should be advanced would depend upon the rate of the sales tax; these factors should be correlated so as to prevent hardship to the lowest income group.

Distributing the Burden of the Sales Tax

In distributing the burden of the sales tax, consideration would be given, of course, not only to the basic rate but also to the effective percentage of tax on the total income. In this connection, Professor Charles O. Hardy, in his pamphlet, *Do We Want a Federal Sales Tax?*[2] presents an interesting table which shows the distribution of the burden of a retail sales tax "designed to produce $5,000,000,000 with exemptions of $200 for each single consumer and $350 for each family," computed on a basic rate of 12.2 per cent.

The table shows that on an income of under $500 the sales tax percentage amounts to 1.6 per cent of the aggregate income (less the exemption); on incomes of $500 to $1,000, 4.8 per cent; on incomes of $1,000 to $1,500, 5.9 per cent; $1,500 to $2,000, 6.2 per cent; $2,000 to $2,500, 6.3 per cent. On incomes of over $2,500 the rate gradually recedes, so that on incomes of $10,000 and over the effective rate is 3.6 per cent.

The tabulations are based on tables prepared by the Office of Price Administration for the Joint Committee on Internal Revenue Taxation.[3] The consumptive expenditures are stated at amounts less housing, medical care, and education. It will thus be seen that these exemptions would greatly reduce the burden on families with incomes in the lowest bracket.

In arriving at a reciprocal relation between the income tax and the retail sales tax, the income tax exemptions should be increased only by such amounts as will coordinate one tax with the other. Conceivably, however, the exemptions would not be increased by amounts in excess of $250 in the case of single persons and $500 for married persons. A resulting

[2] Published by The Brookings Institution, 1943.

[3] *Sales Tax Data, 1942,* pp. 11, 13, 15, 19, 23, 25.

beneficial effect would be that these advances in the income tax exemptions would relieve several million income taxpayers from filing returns.

The argument urged against the sales tax that it inhibits spending becomes an argument in its favor in time of war. In this regard the sales tax is equivalent to a spendings tax without the complexities involved in such taxes. If the Treasury Department is still as friendly to the spendings tax as it has been critical of the sales tax, the urgent need for revenue should be sufficient to reconcile their differences in favor of the retail sales tax.

Productivity of Sales Tax

One of the strongest arguments for the retail sales tax is the fact that it is highly productive. Probably there is no untapped source of taxation which offers to the federal government an equal opportunity for raising substantial revenue. Although retail sales do not offer a rate possibility equal to that of net income, the greater volume possibility should make the retail sales tax as productive of revenue as the tax on net income. It is this vast volume possibility which creates stability and makes retail sales especially attractive as a tax base.

Professor Hardy has cited nine authorities who have estimated the yield of a 10 per cent retail sales tax at from $4,800,000,000 to $6,000,000,000.[4] According to the Treasury Department, a retail sales tax, exempting only sales to the federal, state, and local governments, has been estimated to yield approximately $5,800,000,000.[5] In order, however, that revenues from the income tax shall not be diminished it will

[4] *Do We Want a Federal Sales Tax?* p. 23.

[5] Hearings on the Revenue Act of 1942 before the Ways and Means Committee, 77th Congress, 2nd session, Vol. 1, p. 349.

be necessary to prohibit the deduction of sales tax payments for income tax purposes.

ADMINISTRATION OF SALES TAX

Admittedly the sales tax is susceptible of evasion. A practical solution for the prevention of gross evasion would be to adopt the practice of some states, of requiring all retail merchants to apply for a federal license for which a nominal charge would be made. Such a license would not only serve as a permit to do a retail business, but for administrative purposes it would set up accounting records of those chargeable with the collection of the tax.

Recourse to sales tax records of states employing such a tax would be of inestimable value to the federal government. Such recourse need not be looked upon as an encroachment upon states' rights if the tax by the terms of its enactment by the federal government were limited to the duration of the war.

The cost of administering the retail sales tax is frequently asserted as an obstacle to its profitable employment by the government. Estimates of the cost to the states vary widely—from 1½ per cent to 4 per cent, and in one or two states up to 6 per cent. In view of the background of experience in about one-half the states, it is not unreasonable to expect that the tax could be administered nationally more cheaply than in any state. Since the vendors perform the work of collecting the tax, a few states make a small compensatory allowance for this service. The federal government might do likewise at a small additional cost of collection.

It has been said that there are 2,500,000 retail stores in the United States. Probably one-half the total number are located in states already employing the retail sales tax. But even if sales tax returns were required to be made monthly, the aggregate number, in the course of the year—about 30,000,000—would only be two-thirds the number of income tax returns counted upon this year. Moreover, a sales tax return would be simple in form and calculation as compared with an income tax return since it would be confined to one taxable source.

In an emergency such as the present, when business is running at or close to peak capacity, it would seem highly advisable to require that a retail sales tax should be shifted to the purchaser by separately showing and adding the tax to the sale price. Because of the inflationary possibility it would be highly inadvisable under economic conditions now prevailing to permit the vendor to absorb the tax in the sale price.

Although the retail sales tax, if adopted by the federal government, should be dealt with as in the nature of an experiment, its employment in a period of great emergency appears to be fully justified. The volume of retail sales in the United States is so enormous, even under war restrictions as to manpower and materials, that the productivity of the tax would be assured, and its already successful use by about half the states is an assurance of its practicability as a revenue measure.

Inasmuch as the acceptability of the retail sales tax to the American people would be greatly enhanced if it were enacted as only a temporary measure, its effective period, by provision of the act creating it, should be limited to the duration of the war.

CHAPTER IX

THE SPENDINGS TAX AND THE EXCISES

ALFRED G. BUEHLER

University of Pennsylvania

ON SEPTEMBER 3, 1942, the Treasury presented to the Senate Finance Committee a proposal for a direct, personal, graduated spendings tax, primarily to curb inflation and secondarily to raise revenue. The so-called tax, which was to be refunded in large measure after the war, was to check inflation directly by reducing consumption and by withdrawing purchasing power from consumers, and indirectly, by penalizing spending and rewarding saving. It was emphasized that the spendings tax would be more equitable than a sales tax because it would fall at graduated rates upon spending above the bare subsistence level, that it would not raise prices like a sales tax by entering into costs of production, and that it would be no more difficult of administration than a sales tax.

The Senate Finance Committee and the public were plainly puzzled by this unfamiliar form of taxation. Some observers recalled that the Treasury during World War I had considered the desirability of taxing spendings out of income at a higher rate than savings out of income. After the war Mr. Ogden L. Mills, then a Congressman, in collaboration with Professor T. S. Adams, tax adviser to the Treasury, and Mr. Chester A. Jordan, a businessman, advanced a plan to abandon the surtax on personal incomes for a graduated spendings tax. Few converts were won and the proposal was rejected by Congress.

Tax students are aware that the modern idea of the spendings tax has been in the process of evolution for a long time. Before England adopted her income tax in 1799 she had experimented with a crude form of direct expenditures taxation, which she gave up as a failure. John Stuart Mill, who from time to time urged the withdrawal of the English income tax from all savings, gave credit to an English writer by the name of Revan for introducing the idea in 1847. Mill wanted to tax expenditures out of income, except for a minimum of subsistence, at a flat rate. Realizing that such a tax would give important advantages to persons accumulating wealth, Mill advocated the heavy taxation of property left at death at graduated rates. Living at a time when capital was scarce in relation to investment opportunities, Mill wished to tax consumption rather than saving, hoping to inculcate habits of thrift.

The arguments for the substitution of a tax upon income spent for the conventional income tax which taxes both spending and saving have been made familiar to tax students by Professor Irving Fisher in this country and by him and other economists, under the influence of Mill, in Italy and Germany, who are convinced that consumer expenditures provide the only true and objective measure of income for taxation. Before 1913 Fisher and others had argued that an income tax should not be applied to capital gains and savings in other forms, but these pleas produced few noticeable effects upon the methods of income taxation in this country. On this particular occasion, our interest is focused upon the graduated spendings tax as an extension of, and not as a substitute for, the personal income tax, and upon this tax as a temporary war measure rather than as a normal revenue and regulator of saving.

The novelty of the Treasury proposal was the scheme to employ the spendings tax as a device to ration consumer purchasing power, while raising revenue, in combination with other measures to curb inflation. Fiscal controls were thus to supplement rationing and price ceilings in striking at the roots of inflation as it was engendered by the expenditure of excess consumer purchasing power. Considerable revenue would be raised if the plan were adopted, and whether it was accepted or not, the rush in Congress to a sales tax might be stemmed.

The arguments for the spendings tax as a fiscal device to check inflation have been stated in the official papers of Treasury spokesmen and in the unofficial papers of the Treasury economists. It was apparently assumed at the outset that fiscal policy in wartime should be motivated by the purposes: (1) to encourage the greatest possible production, particularly for war needs; (2) to distribute the available consumer goods as equitably as possible; and (3) to facilitate postwar readjustment by curbing inflation during the war and afterward. The compelling considerations in favor of the spendings tax rather than other alternatives to promote these objectives were (1) that it would penalize consumer spending not required to provide basic necessities while inducing saving; (2) that it would discourage the spending of funds already accumulated; and (3) that it would not deaden the incentives to work, produce, and save as further stiff increases in the income tax might, since the spendings tax would fall upon spending rather than upon saving, and it would largely be refunded after the war.

Treasury spokesmen have emphasized the point that a graduated spendings tax would be a flexible instrument of fiscal control which could be personalized to a high degree with its exemptions, deductions, and graduated rates. The very poor would be entirely exempt from the tax and the tax rates upon the successive brackets of spending would rise progressively to the desired maximum. In fact, the rates could be elevated to the point that they would throttle consumption above a certain level. The tax offered an attractive alternative to the general rationing of consumer purchasing power. It would lessen the need for more stringent direct controls and would strengthen the limited rationing and price controls.

Quite incidentally, the Treasury implied, the spendings tax would raise approximately $6 billion in new revenue—a very large sum for a tax offered primarily as a nonrevenue measure. The equitable burdens of the tax were contrasted with the unequal and regressive burdens of a sales tax.

The administration of the proposed spendings tax would be no more difficult than the administration of a sales tax, the Treasury maintained, because the spendings tax could be collected as an extension of the income tax without an unreasonable amount of additional labor and expense. A sales tax, on the other hand, would require a new administrative unit and many thousands of new employees for its collection.

The theoretical advantages of a graduated spendings tax as a device to curb inflation are apparent to the thoughtful student of taxation and many economists have glowed with enthusiasm over this remarkable fiscal invention. The tax, if successfully enforced, would tend to direct consumers' funds away from dangerous spending into savings. Much or all of the tax could be refunded after the war at a propitious time to release funds for consumer spending when depression and unemployment threatened. As a flexible fiscal control, equitably applied, it would seem admirably suited to wartime conditions, when the threat of inflation is always present.

Reception of Treasury Proposal

If the graduated spendings tax promises such important advantages as a major feature of an anti-inflation program, why was it not immediately adopted by Congress? Why was the spendings tax dropped from the Treasury tax program in 1943?

The spendings tax was recommended to the Senate Finance Committee, in a closed executive session, after the Treasury had given it passing praise in a memorandum issued to the Ways and Means Committee in one of its closed sessions. There had been little or no popular discussion of the spendings tax, which had no great popular following. The public was unaware that the Treasury had considered the tax for several months, and the tax had not been recommended to the public by the President. Thus, without an effective build-up campaign, the tax had been released to the Senate Finance Committee.

The members of the Senate Finance Committee were, for the most part, either indifferent or hostile to the proposal. Many of the members of Congress were warmly advocating a sales tax, and this sentiment was evident in the Committee. The Committee members professed an inability to understand the Treasury proposal. The tax was to be levied at very high rates, ranging upward to 85 per cent, which appeared confiscatory to some observers. Perhaps a more moderate tax would have won more supporters. The tax was to be superimposed upon the already complex personal income tax and taxation would become more, rather than less, complex.

Experience in the collection of a graduated spendings tax was lacking both here and abroad. While our experience with the income tax would be very valuable in the administration of a spendings tax, the latter would introduce new problems and its adoption would strain still further the machinery of income tax enforcement, and its failure would inevitably discredit the income tax.

It was evident, moreover, that neither Congress nor the public was prepared to accept an all-out program of expenditure rationing. The dangers of inflation seemed remote and the country was willing to follow the easy path and take only moderate precautions against those dangers.

The spendings tax proposed by the Treasury seemed hopelessly complicated to many observers familiar with the temper of the taxpayers. The tax consisted of two features, one a so-called tax at a flat rate of 10 per cent upon total individual expenditures, to be imposed in such a way that it would not reduce the tax-free expenditures of a single person below $500 and those of a married couple below $1,000, with an allowance of $250 for each dependent. This part of the tax, which was to raise an estimated $4.5 billion, was to be refunded to the taxpayers, without interest, after the war. It was really a forced loan.

An additional spendings tax, a surtax, was to be collected at rates graduated from 10 to 75 per cent. It was not to be refunded and it was to yield approximately $1.5 billion. For this tax, a single person would be allowed an exemption of $1,000 and a married couple $2,000, with a credit of $500 for each dependent. The spendings bracket of a married couple would be twice as large as that of a single person, and each dependent would be allowed a bracket half as large as a single person. This all seemed very confusing to the senators and the public.

The spendings taxes were to be collected in conjunction with the personal income tax. For the surtax, expenditures would be reported quarterly, with a final adjustment at the end of the year. In order to compute their spendings taxes the individual spenders would have to report in some detail their expenditures during the year. Possibly a simplified tax form would eventually have developed for the smaller taxpayers. Instead of asking the taxpayers to account for their expenditures item by item or category by category, the taxpayers would be asked to supplement the information on their income tax return with a declaration of the total funds at their disposal during the year, from which they would deduct their itemized savings, debt payments, and other permissible uses of funds. The remainder, it would be assumed, would be the total expenditures during the year.

The process of computation may be illustrated by an examination of the attached schedule, which was suggested by the Treasury for the use of the taxpayers. By following the instructions, through a process of addition of disposable funds and the subtraction of deductible uses of funds, the taxpayer would finally ascertain his estimated yearly expenditures.

To those who inspect this schedule in a calmly rational manner, its arithmetic requirements, while something of a nuisance, do not seem to be insurmountable. But both Congress and the public greeted the proposed schedule with anything but eagerness. In fact, the abhorrence for the work required to fill out the form[1] was evident to those who ob-

[1] THE TREASURY'S INDIVIDUAL SPENDINGS TAX SCHEDULE

This would be used by those subject to the spendings surtax, i.e., single persons with spendings above an exemption of $1,000 and heads of families with spendings above an exemption of $2,000, with $500 additional exempt for each dependent. For other taxpayers, a simplified schedule would be available.

FUNDS AT THE DISPOSAL OF THE INDIVIDUAL:

1. Salaries, wages, and other compensation for personal services....$
2. Dividends and interest received, including government interest..
3. Rents, royalties, annuities, pensions..........................
4. Withdrawals from business, professions, partnerships, trusts....
5. Cash receipts from gifts, bequests, and insurance.............
6. Receipts from sale of capital assets..........................
7. Receipts from repayment of loans made to others............

served the grimaces and explosive remarks of many of the indignant taxpayers who gave the matter any thought. In our democratic form of government, it is extremely unlikely that a tax which appears highly complex and which wins little popular support will be forced upon the taxpayers by Congress, whatever advantages it may offer as an antidote to the poison of inflation, especially when the nation has not been aroused to appreciate the menace of the threatened flood of inflation.

Problems of the Spendings Tax

The problems of the spendings tax, on the other hand, are neither few nor simple. The Treasury, perforce by circumstance, proposed a plan not fully worked out, with features bound to create controversy. Here we can mention only a few of the problems encountered in the attempt to define and tax consumer expenditures. One of the problems is that of exemptions and credits. Economists would perhaps generally agree that at least the bare subsistence expenditures of the lowest incomes should be exempt. Then how may we define

---

8. Receipts from borrowing, including debts incurred on installment purchases.....................................
9. Cash and bank balances at beginning of year..................
10. Other receipts..
11. TOTAL DISPOSABLE FUNDS (Items 1 to 10) ....$

DEDUCTIONS: NON-TAXABLE USE OF FUNDS:

12. Cash and bank balances at end of year......................$
13. Cash gifts and contributions...............................
14. Interest and taxes paid, except on owner-occupied homes......
15. Expenditures on the purchase of capital assets................
16. Life insurance premiums, annuity, and pension payments......
17. Outlays for repayment of debt, including installment debt.....
18. Loans made to others..
19. Other non-taxable disbursements............................
20. TOTAL DEDUCTIONS (Items 12 to 19) ....$
21. EXPENDITURES SUBJECT TO TAX (Item 11 minus item 20) ....$

the minimum of subsistence, remembering that living costs vary in different sections of the country, that farm families usually produce much of their food and city families usually buy nearly all of their food, that spending patterns vary among different income levels, among different parts of the country, and among different families, and that hardship cases will result from the application of arbitrary and uniform exemptions?

In fixing the exemptions the problems of curbing inflation and the revenue needs of the government must not be ignored. If the exemptions are as low as a control program would require, will the population accept them and will they be feasible of administration? These and many other questions are bound to arise. They may not be insuperable but they do present some difficult political and economic complications.

The effectiveness of a tax designed to check inflation by burdening consumption expenditures will be enhanced if the tax can be applied to all spending from income, as well as from nonincome, sources, excepting only the sources which are exempt. A spendings tax would provide a broader tax base than a retail sales tax because it would probably fall upon purchases of services while a sales tax would probably impinge upon spending for few if any services, which might, however, be taxed to some extent with excises. On the other hand, a retail sales tax would hit spending for commodities from past savings quite effectively but a spendings tax could be evaded rather easily by not reporting the spending of savings.

Individual cash hoarding is not an inflationary menace so long as the accumulated funds are withheld from the markets until the scarcity of supplies can be relieved. A graduated spendings tax would encourage saving and discourage spending, especially if its rates were high, but it would not necessarily encourage the investment of savings in war loans or in productive investments instead of hoarding, unless the deductions were arranged to discriminate against hoarding.

The Treasury plan required the individual to declare his holdings in cash at the outset. Increases in cash and in other savings would be deductible, spendings out of cash and other savings would be taxable. But how could the Treasury be certain that hoards of cash would be reported when the tax became operative? It would have to rely very largely upon the veracity of the taxpayers, and the dishonest could be caught only with the greatest difficulty, especially if they were numerous, as they might be. The tax dodgers would also report fictitious increases in savings and spend their funds, but they would have to report their outlets for savings, and this would tend to stop evasion. The honest could avoid part of the spendings tax by hoarding or saving otherwise, waiting to spend until the tax should expire; or they could purchase free from the tax, in so far as they had funds, before it became operative. If the tax remained long in effect, some of the opportunities for evasion and avoidance would automatically close or be discovered.

To be effective as an inflationary curb, the tax would have to remain and be strictly enforced until the threat of inflation had disappeared some time after the war. The difficulties of checking cash on hand would always be present and it would seem desirable for society to discourage the accumulation of large cash hoards when funds are needed for investment in war loans. In view of these facts, would it not be wise to disallow more than a nominal amount of cash as a deduction? To prevent the dangerous dishoarding of funds on a vast scale during and after the war, should not savings be placed in nonnegotiable government and nongovernment investments, except for extreme emergency needs?

Further questions arise concerning deductions for various forms of savings, which the Treasury proposal would treat uniformly. Would it be desirable and feasible to discriminate in the deductions against payments on freshly incurred debts, loans to other persons, and other forms of saving as well as increases in cash, and to give the fullest allowances for war bond purchases and certain other restricted investments? These questions must be considered and answers must be found for them if the spendings tax is to operate most effectively against inflation and if its application is to be equitable and practicable.

Another complex problem is encountered in the treatment of housing expenses. Should expenditures for the purchase of homes, including interest, taxes on homes, rentals paid for living quarters, and imputed rentals for owner-occupied dwellings be allowed fully or in some measure as deductions? The Treasury proposed to permit no deduction for taxes, interest, or rentals actually paid. No effort was to be made, however, to tax imputed rentals, apparently because of the great difficulties faced in the imputation process. The deductions permitted in the income tax for interest and taxes on homes were to be denied in the spendings tax because payments on debts were to be deductible, and out of fairness to tenants, who would receive no deduction for rentals, it was felt that interest and taxes should not be deductible. Homeowners, moreover, would pay the spendings tax upon expenditures for repairs, fuel, and many other housing expenses.

This compromise did not appear to be entirely satisfactory to taxpayers. Unless imputed rentals could be taxed, it would seem unfair to tax rentals actually paid. The practical obstacles to imputation would seem to rule that out, and that would probably mean that rentals paid could not be taxed either. Public opinion would probably be the guiding factor here, and it might demand that all rentals, imputed and paid, and debt payments, interest, and taxes should be excluded.

There would still remain the housing expenses incurred by owners for repairs, fuel, and other items which might be included in the rentals charged to tenants. Would public opinion require deductions for them also? The Treasury plan would not seem to offer a final answer for the perplexing problems created by housing expenditures. These problems are of such importance that a reasonably equitable, practicable, and popular compromise would have to be worked out if a spendings tax were to be adopted and to remain long in force. Otherwise storms of popular disapproval would be invited.

Other complex problems would be encountered. How should gifts, contributions, and bequests be treated? How should capital assets be defined? What provisions would be necessary to deal with unusual cases of hardship? How serious would the inequities of the tax be, because of evasion and avoidance? Would the regressive effects of the flat refundable tax prove to be of serious consequence, or would the promised refunding allay the complaints of the taxpayers?

One of the important issues raised by the proposed spendings tax was the question of forced loans, which has many interesting angles. If a consumption tax is to be refunded in large measure, would a refundable sales tax, like that proposed by Senator Danaher, be more convenient and practicable? A fundamental fiscal question must be answered, why should any part of the tax be refunded? Why not face the music and pay outright taxes once and for all? How could the spendings tax be refunded after the war, considering the powerful political pressure which the taxpayers could exert, without creating or maintaining an inflationary boom? What would be the economic effects of refunding about three-fourths of the spendings tax collections? These are only a few of the problems presented by the proposal to employ the spendings tax as a device to collect forced war loans.

Administration of a Spendings Tax

In noting some of the more pressing problems of the spendings tax, we should not pass over lightly its administrative problems, which the Treasury argued would not be unduly serious and would not be of greater magnitude than the problems of administering a sales tax. For the successful enforcement of the tax, as already stated, the Treasury would require a rather full accounting by the taxpayers of their total disposable funds and their deductions. It would have to depend very largely upon the taxpayers for the intelligent and honest reporting of the essential facts.

Many opportunities for tax evasion would be offered because of the numerous sources of spendable funds and the various deductions, and the difficulties involved in the checking of the returns would be more numerous than in the checking for the income tax. The inducements to tax evasion would be material also because of the high tax rates. The administration of a direct, graduated, personal spendings tax, imposed upon the great mass of the population, would encounter all of the problems of income tax administration and many more. Of all taxes, it would require enthusiastic popular support and cooperation. If a considerable part of the taxpaying public met the tax with great indifference or with open opposition, its failure would seem certain.

I have talked with many individuals about the spendings tax and its compliance problems, including workers, farmers, clerks, professional and business people, housewives, and others. Few of these have evinced any serious desire to cooperate in giving the Treasury the information needed for its enforcement. Many would regard the request for information an inquisition. No doubt, however, if a spendings tax were placed upon the statute books many of these would at least go through the motions of furnishing the necessary data, but their hearts would not be in the unpleasant task of digging up and giving out this information.

A number of economists have told me that they would be glad to go along with the Treasury in an experiment in spendings taxation because they realize the dangers of inflation, they feel a graduated spendings tax would help in curbing it, and they believe it would be reasonably equitable. A few tax accountants and lawyers have told me that they thought a spendings tax could be enforced successfully, but many more have doubted it. I have also found little conviction among tax administrators that enforcement at this time would be practicable.

Doubtless many of those who regard a spendings tax as impracticable are opposed to it, and their bias has influenced their conclusion. But the unwillingness to go along with the Treasury on a spendings tax seems to be so universal that it must be accepted as a great and real obstacle to both its adoption and its enforcement, however one may explain that reluctance.

Economic Effects of Spendings Tax

If one wishes to wave away, for the sake of the discussion, the practical obstacles to the introduction of a graduated spendings tax in the financing of World War II, and if it is assumed that the tax becomes fully feasible, it could become a powerful brake upon inflationary consumer spending. It might, to some extent, be paid by sacrificing saving rather than spending, however, among those who deemed it necessary or desirable to maintain a level of living which could be supported only by giving up saving to pay part or all of the tax.

Would a spendings tax which exempted only the subsistence expenditures of the lowest income group have any inflationary effects, or would it be accepted as a necessary war sacrifice without demands for higher compensation? The Treasury appeared to feel that the tax would have few, if any, incidental inflationary effects. It should be noted, however, that the tax would not exempt the subsistence expenditures of a great part of the population and that the labor and farm organizations expressed no warm public approval of it. Its inflationary tendencies would be lessened by the promise of a refund of most of the tax after the war, but this might not stave off vigorous demands for higher wages and farm incomes if the tax should be adopted.

When the Treasury proposed its increased income tax in 1943, much of which would be refunded after the war, representatives of the CIO, including President Murray, expressed strong disapproval. Mr. Murray indicated that his organization would regard the levy of the increased income tax inimical to organized labor and that its enactment would be the signal for a drive to increase wages in order to meet the higher cost of living. The adoption of the Treasury spendings tax would probably have a similar effect, and the tax might precipitate vigorous agitation by the farm and labor groups for higher incomes. These groups did not ask for the spendings tax, they have sought to escape the effects of higher living costs and taxes, and it is not unlikely that they would feel inclined to meet its inroads upon their purchasing power with requests for concessions to offset it.

To some extent a graduated spendings tax, depending upon the reactions of organized groups and their influence, might therefore act to raise costs and prices. On balance, it should act to diminish, rather than to increase inflation, depending on the operation of variable factors, but its anti-inflationary effects should not be overlooked.

In the long run, a graduated spendings tax would tend to encourage thrift and discourage spending. Its usefulness would therefore, depend upon the desirability of lessening spending and increasing saving. In wartime it is especially desirable to promote saving and to limit and direct consumption. In this program a spendings tax, if practicable, would be a very useful and effective fiscal instrument. Its role in peacetime, under other conditions, is another matter.

Because of the many problems attendant upon the introduction and enforcement of a graduated spendings tax, it should not be adopted in haste as a brief measure. It would probably require a few years at least to discover and smooth out its difficulties, and its effectiveness in curbing inflation would be impaired if it were not continued after the war until the menace of inflation had passed. The graduated spendings tax does not appear to be an available fiscal instrument for curbing present inflationary tendencies. Experimentation in its use must be postponed until another emergency is presented and the population is willing to undertake the experiment.

Alternative Tax on Uninvested Income

After a discussion of the deficiencies of the income tax in wartime, instead of adopting a spendings tax or a sales tax, Congress introduced the Victory tax. The Treasury spokesmen and others had indicated that further increases in the income tax would rest heavily upon those with debts and other contractual obligations. As a concession to certain forms of saving and a compromise with the various gross income tax, spendings tax, and other proposals, the Victory tax was designed to fall upon income after restricted savings had been deducted. The hybrid tax was neither fish nor fowl; it seemed to please no one completely.

If the Treasury, when it presented its spendings tax, had sensed the impossibility of securing the spendings tax and had been willing to go along with Congress in planning a new income tax with full allowances for socially desirable forms of saving, perhaps largely excluding cash accumulations, it might have obtained an additional tax levied upon uninvested income. This would have taxed spending from income at graduated rates and it would also have passed over lightly the taxpayers with debt payments and other fixed obligations.

Such a tax would not reach spending out of capital, like a well enforced spendings tax. On the other hand, the spendings tax, especially at the outset, might fall considerably short of this goal, and spending out of capital could be hit with excises or a sales tax.

A tax upon net income, with deductions for investments out of income, should be intelligible to the average American, with his impatience for tax details. In addition to his net income, which he would have to report anyway, he would report only a limited list of deductions, with sufficient details for the Treasury to check. His inducement to report deductions would be his tax saving, which might, in fact, invite some false reporting. The tax would demand additional compliance and administrative work, but not so much as the spendings tax.

The tax could be arranged, by disallowing deductions for cash accumulation, to discourage hoarding. It would not offer all of the theoretical advantages of the spendings tax, but it would offer a number of them and it should be simpler and more practicable. It might be found to be an effective supplementary tax control over much of the inflationary spending, especially in conjunction with a well developed excise tax program.

The Excises

Thus far I have merely mentioned the excises, or the federal internal commodity taxes which are directed toward consumption. Such taxes have long been employed in this country for both war and peace revenues. In fact much of their development has occurred during the Civil War and the later conflicts. The excises have proved to be useful vehicles for gathering into the Treasury large portions of the consumers' spending power. They have been looked upon primarily as revenues and they have not been developed to any great extent as regulators of consumption along particular lines.

According to recent Treasury estimates, the various excises will return approximately $4,274 million in the fiscal year ending June 30, 1944, excluding the new excises in the 1944 revenue law, or approximately one-tenth of the gross tax revenues. The alcoholic beverage taxes will yield about $1,509 million, the tobacco taxes $988 million, the retailers' excises $184 million, the admissions tax $179 million, the tax on transportation of persons $171 million, and the gasoline tax $273 million. The remainder will be derived from various excises.

Some of the commodities and services taxed are employed in production, others are utilized almost exclusively in consumption. The various excises, sales taxes, and customs duties in this country do not, in the aggregate, provide as relatively great revenues as the combined commodity taxes of the other leading English speaking nations. In the fiscal year 1942-1943, the percentages of total central and non-central government tax revenues derived from all categories of commodity taxes in this and other countries were as follows:

Australia	37
Canada	32
United Kingdom	30
United States	19

For the rigid control of consumer expenditures upon particular commodities and services which may be required in the war effort, or which are produced in competition with war materials, direct physical controls will probably prove to be more effective, more convenient of administration, and more equitable than commodity taxes. If scarce commodities are to be rationed among the population, this cannot be accomplished equitably by placing heavy excises upon the articles and trusting the resultant price increases to apportion the articles fairly, because those with the greater funds can better afford to pay the higher prices, regardless of their needs. Nor will it be certain that those possessing purchasing power will be able to procure the scarce goods.

The excises cannot be personalized sufficiently in their application to permit a highly individualized program of consumption control. Many of them fall upon commodities employed in both war and nonwar production and enter into prices directly. Some of them, to be sure, like the taxes upon tobacco and admissions, fall largely upon civilian consumption. The taxes upon consumption will not directly reduce the demand for articles competing with the war effort unless the demand for them is quite elastic and declines sharply when the tax is imposed, or the tax is so heavy that it suppresses consumption.

The excises can be employed, however, to absorb excessive

consumer purchasing power rather effectively if they are placed upon commodities purchased by those with a surplus of expendable funds. They may thus supplement other tax and direct controls in the program against inflation. They tend, in general, to reward saving and to penalize spending, but like a spendings or sales tax they may reduce savings more or less.

In order to avoid onerous burdens upon subsistence and not to dull incentives to work, the excises should, so far as possible, exempt absolute necessities. Their regressive effects can be softened by lifting them, where possible, from the lowest incomes. On the other hand, they will not serve effectively to divert large amounts of mass purchasing power from the markets unless they are levied upon commodities consumed by the masses.

The excises may exert inflationary effects as they raise costs and prices along the line. To minimize these effects, they should be collected as close to the consumer as possible, that is, at the retail level, and they should not be imposed upon commodities employed in production. Taxes upon retailing may be less convenient to administer than taxes upon manufacturing, however, and the retailers may also object to them. The opposition of the retailers may be eased by making the taxes convenient to compute, with a saving in compliance costs. Like other consumption taxes, they provide material for organized labor, the farmers, and others to argue for higher rewards. In general, however, they will probably act to reduce, rather than to increase, inflationary pressure.

Heavier Excises Desirable

One is inclined to remark here that if the inflationary possibilities of income, spendings, and excise taxes are to be minimized, the taxpayers who feel their burdens must look upon them as necessary sacrifices for the successful prosecution of the war which help to distribute the costs of war equitably. If war taxes are compensated for in higher remuneration, war contributions become meaningless.

I believe that we could extend our excises to advantage still further beyond the increases in the 1944 law. On many commodities we are paying lower tax rates than are being paid in other countries. It is true that the difficulties of raising more revenue from consumers' excess funds increase as the taxes increase because of the political pressures brought into play, and that the taxes may impose many unequal burdens. But we refused to enact a spendings or sales tax and we have fought off steep increases in the income tax, at a time when much dangerous spending power is in existence. The excises are far from perfect devices for the absorption of consumer funds, but they will help in the battle against inflation. We should, therefore, seek ways and means to increase the rates of existing excises and to impose new excises where it is found that considerable revenue can be drained out of bulging consumers' purses without serious damage to essential consumption.

CHAPTER X

THE INDIVIDUAL INCOME TAX AS A METHOD OF INFLATION CONTROL

ROY BLOUGH

Director of Tax Research, Treasury Department

SOME PEOPLE who oppose the use of taxation for any purpose other than the raising of revenue object to its use as an instrument of inflation control. Aside from the basic question of what are the proper uses of taxation, it may be observed that the purpose of raising revenue is itself closely tied up with inflation control. Underlying the purpose of raising revenue is a more fundamental purpose, that of avoiding the harmful effects which would follow if expenditures were indefinitely financed without taxation—which in general would mean using the printing press or the banks as the source of funds. If such methods of financing produced no ill effects there would be no reason for the hair shirt of taxation. But such methods do produce ill effects, of which the most spectacular and perhaps the most important is inflation. Over the centuries, the desirability of taxation as a source of funds has become somewhat detached from its underlying rationale and has acquired an authority of its own. At bottom, however, a fundamental objective of taxation, which largely determines the validity of the revenue objective, is the prevention and control of present and future inflation.

PRELIMINARY ASSUMPTIONS CONCERNING INFLATION

Accordingly, no apologies are necessary in considering taxation as a means of inflation control. Before proceeding to the discussion of the individual income tax as a method of inflation control, an introductory summary statement of certain conclusions about inflation, which for the present purposes serve as assumptions, may be found helpful.

1. Inflation, used here as synonymous with inflationary price rise, is not a curse visited by some supernatural power but grows out of human institutions and human actions and is therefore preventable and controllable if people, especially people in organized groups, understand its causes and phases and are willing to take the steps necessary to prevent and control it.

2. Inflation is characterized by a situation where consumers and business organizations are able and attempt to buy more goods and services than are available under conditions where the normal mechanisms for increasing supply and limiting demand are not operative, owing to restrictions on increases in the supply of goods financially accompanied by continued additions to the volume of spendable funds.[1]

3. By inflation control is meant the deliberate action of an organized society to prevent, delay, or limit inflationary price rises through removal of the restrictions on supply and of additions to spending power that cause such price rises, or through modification of their impact on prices.

4. Some control measures are:

   a. Increasing the supplies of civilian goods through increased efficiency, increased use of natural and human resources, improved transportation and increased imports, as well as by diversion of resources from other uses.

   b. Decreasing, or limiting the increase, of spendable funds by (1) limitation of governmental expenditures which tend to increase such funds, (2) checking growth of income by control of wages, trade margins, and farm prices, (3) reduction or limitation of credit expansion for private purposes, and (4) appropriate taxation and borrowing measures.

---

[1] The restrictions are often not complete and the additions not unlimited, so that inflations are usually self-limiting without conscious control methods.

c. Reducing or limiting the efforts of consumers and business concerns to spend current income and accumulated savings, through priorities, rationing, patriotic appeals, and through a policy of preventing price increases by directive.

5. Legal limitation of price, although a useful measure of control in avoiding increases in efforts to spend available funds, can be fully effective only temporarily if inflationary forces continue or other control measures are not taken.

6. Heavy taxation, although by no means the only method needed for inflation control when inflationary pressures are great, is a basic method which (a) reduces spendable funds, thus striking directly at causes, (b) encourages private loans to government by indicating the serious intention of government to control inflation, and (c) if applied on a rising scale which the spending public believes will continue to rise, discourages spending because of anticipation of higher taxes.

7. Different forms of taxation may be considered alternative or complementary for the purposes of inflation control. If all taxes have the same anti-inflationary influence per dollar of collections, the control of inflation is not a consideration in comparing the desirability of taxes; but if the effects are different, the control of inflation becomes a consideration in comparing the desirability of different taxes in a period when inflation control is desired. For policy purposes it cannot be assumed without evidence or demonstration that different taxes and different rate schedules producing the same revenue will have equal anti-inflationary effects.

The foregoing summary is not intended to be complete; it is intended rather as general background.

This paper is directed to a consideration of the factors affecting the anti-inflationary effects of the individual income tax. By "individual income tax" is meant a tax on individual net income above personal exemptions and credits for dependents such as is imposed by the federal government. In general, this paper does not proceed to the stage of comparing the anti-inflationary effects of the individual income tax with those of other taxes.

Effectiveness in Reaching Income

Since current income is the principal source of spendable funds, one factor determining the effectiveness of a tax is the extent to which it is able to reach income. The individual income tax does not reach all income; some income is excluded from computation of the tax and some is eliminated through deductions, while personal exemptions and credits for dependents reduce the balance.

Under war conditions, with total income payments to individual citizens running about $150 billion annually, roughly $35 billion is removed from the tax base by "exclusions" (chiefly the tax-free allowance of $1,500 per annum for members of the armed forces) and deductions for interest, taxes, extraordinary medical expenses, contributions, etc. This leaves a net income, in the sense of the income tax law, of roughly $115 billion.

Of this $115 billion, about $60 billion is taken out of the tax base, chiefly through the personal exemptions and credits for dependents claimed by those subject to tax, though the figure also includes the total net income of persons who are not taxable because their exemptions and credits for dependents exceed their net income. The remaining $55 billion (between 35 and 40 per cent of total income payments) is the amount subject to the regular income tax. A considerably greater amount is subject to Victory tax, in view of the much smaller exemption allowed heads of families under that tax; but since the Victory tax rate of 3 per cent is so low compared with normal tax and surtax, this special-purpose addition to the tax base contributes little to revenue or anti-inflation effects. Less than $300 million of tax is expected to be paid at 1944 income levels by persons subject to Victory tax who are below the exemption levels of the regular tax.

While the tax base under the income tax is very much

smaller than the total national income, it is still sufficient to make the income tax very effective. The principle of exempting the taxpayer's bottom dollars makes sense not only from the standpoint of fairness but also from the standpoint of directing our measures against inflation to the right address. As was just mentioned, the greater part of the income which disappears from the tax base represents exemptions and credits for dependents. Most of the income so exempted is required to support taxpayers and their dependents at the minimum level for health and working efficiency. Admitting that inflationary pressure might be less if more citizens were so poor that they could not reach this minimum standard, it is still appropriate that pressure to reduce spending should be applied only to the excess over minimum standards.

Needless to say, there is no perfectly satisfactory way of deciding how much is essential; and under wartime conditions, it is necessary to be less generous in gauging essentials than in normal times. If a larger tax base is needed, it can be obtained under the income tax by less generous treatment of the types of income now excluded and deducted, and by reduction of income tax exemptions. Even if lowering exemptions means that some part of the necessary minimum is taxed, this can be defended as preferable to going over to types of taxes whose base includes the entire necessary minimum.

No exemption system can ever be perfect; ours certainly is not. The necessary minimum which has a claim to be protected from taxation undoubtedly varies according to occupation, length of the work week, previous living standard, and similar factors. There are also very important differences in the standard of living which a given amount of money income can support. Dollar for dollar of statutory net income, a farm family can enjoy a more adequate standard of living than can a small town family, which in turn can support a more adequate standard than a city family. At the city end of the scale, less people are able to raise their own food. More are obliged to live in rented houses or apartments; and for those who rent, rents are higher. Furthermore, what is considered an "adequate" standard of living is on the whole more elaborate in large cities than small towns or in the country. Thus, a level of personal exemptions and credits for dependents which is too low to keep up working efficiency in an industrial city might simultaneously be more than adequate in small towns and country areas.

Another factor bearing on the adequacy of personal exemptions is that families differ very much in their make-up and in the number of persons who contribute to family support. In families where several adult members contribute their earnings, the total amount of untaxed income for the family as a whole may be very much larger than where all the income is earned by husband and wife. On the other hand, as between families where both husband and wife are at work and families where only husbands work, and where total income is the same, the family which enjoys the wife's services as full-time housekeeper is plainly better off; but no offset to this advantage is offered by our present tax system (except a difference of less than $20 of liability under the Victory tax).

Timing of Payment

The effectiveness of a tax as an anti-inflationary device is determined in part by the timing of payment. If, for example, incomes generally increase by 25 or 50 per cent in the course of a year and the taxes are not collected until the year following receipt of income, the current effect on spending will be less than if the tax is collected immediately. The prospect of payment in the following year has a restraining effect on spending in the current year but not to nearly the same extent as current payment, which removes the ability to spend.

Up to the past few months, the individual income tax collections have lagged by as much as a year behind the receipt of income. Under the present current payment act the timing is much closer although it is not yet perfect. That portion of the tax that is withheld at source is withheld concurrently with the payment of the income and never reaches the hands of the consumer. The rest of the tax is to be paid in quarterly installments near the end of each quarter. These installments are not based on the income of the quarter but are supposed to represent one-quarter of the estimated tax for the whole year. Because of the nature of this estimated tax system there is not adequate provision to prevent some postponement of payment. One-fifth may be paid without penalty in the following March instead of during the current year. There is now no penalty for underestimate and underpayment during the current year if quarterly installments are paid based on income at least as large as that of the previous year. Protection is not adequate against allowing the tax liability to accumulate during the year and to be paid largely in the latter half of the year. Specific provision is made to permit farmers to pay no tax before December 15, to pay as little as two-thirds at that time, and to pay one-third the following March 15.

Despite the exceptions, however, if the purpose and spirit of the present law are carried out in operation, the timing of the income tax payments is satisfactorily coordinated with the timing of the receipt of income.

Tax rates can now be raised or lowered at any time during the year, making the income tax available as an adjustable tax to meet changes in inflationary requirements. Even leaving aside the political problems of such adjustments, however, the flexibility is not as great as appears on the surface. For income withheld at source there is no great problem in increasing the rate of withholding within a period of thirty or sixty days after the change in law is passed. With respect to the estimated tax the change would involve a new estimation by all taxpayers subject to making the declaration of estimated tax. This is not impossible but would enlarge the not inconsiderable compliance problems of existing law. Moreover, changing the rate of tax during the year increases complications and imposes a handicap on tax simplification.

Effects on Spending and Saving

The effectiveness of various dollars of income tax in reducing spending varies from person to person. No attempt will be made here to go into all of the variations in situations which may cause a dollar of tax to reduce saving or spending as the case may be. In general, an additional dollar in tax would reduce spending more in the case of a person with a low income than of a person with a high income since the margin for saving is much less. Persons subject to the income tax (not including the Victory tax) account for roughly three-fourths of the total expenditures. In view of the fact that the exempt part of income does not in most cases materially exceed a necessary minimum, the persons reached by the income tax must be considered the source of virtually all the "excess" expenditures, over and above necessities, which can safely be cut when inflation danger compels a contraction.

Spendings may be made from accumulated savings as well as from current income, and such savings are an important source of funds for normal purchases. In addition to these normal purchases the accumulated savings of the past few years constitute a substantial threat to prices in case there should be anything approaching a mass movement of the use of such savings for the purchase of goods and services. The income tax places no penalty on the spending of accumulated savings and does not operate to freeze such savings, although it does reduce the further accumulation of savings.

In addition to the effects of taxes on the ability of persons to buy are the effects on their willingness or decision to buy assuming they have the ability. The income tax does not place any special penalties on the expenditure of money and accordingly does not discourage spending except in so far as it reduces the amount available to be spent.

Effects on Wages, etc.

Another factor in determining the effectiveness of a tax as an anti-inflationary instrument is the extent to which it results in pressure for higher income. Specifically, there is always the danger that the imposition of an increased tax will result in so much additional pressure for higher wages that the actual reduction in income achieved by the tax will be much smaller than the amount of the tax and may in fact be negative. Moreover, the higher wages would not only contribute income to the spending stream but would increase the costs of doing business and thus force price ceilings to be raised, thereby reducing the effectiveness of various price and inflation control devices.

Different aspects of the individual income tax work in opposite directions with respect to the effect on the demand for higher wages and salaries. The pressure is reduced by the fact that the income tax has personal exemptions which protect from the higher tax a minimum standard of living. Moreover, the exemptions differ from person to person depending on family status. A unified demand for higher wages is less likely to develop among people who are differently affected by a tax than among people who are uniformly affected by the tax. The income tax, moreover, is a direct tax and is recognized as being intended to fall on those with income. Less excuse is offered for demanding offsetting income increases than where the tax is indirect. Moreover, the exemption and progressive rate features of the tax give it a fairness in application which undoubtedly reduces the hostility of workers towards rate increases.

On the other hand, the income tax on workers is for the most part collected through the withholding of tax at source by the employer. The result of an increase in tax is thus to reduce the amount in the pay envelope. The effect of the tax on the spendable income is very direct and is brought immediately to the attention of the employee. Moreover, the apparent reduction in income may be blamed emotionally on the employer even though the worker knows that the employer has no choice in the matter. The reduction of pay in the form of increased withholding would likely be a substantial influence in the direction of demand for higher wages, and much more so than if the tax were not due until the following year. In the latter case the separation of the date of receiving the income from the date of paying the tax would, at least to some extent, separate them in the mind of the taxpayer and give him less immediate cause for demanding higher pay. Of course, when the tax came due in a lump sum, the worker's reaction might be accentuated, even though postponed.

With a highly organized labor movement, a good deal of the effect of tax increases on demand for wage increases will depend on how labor leaders feel and what educational campaigns they undertake with their members. Of course, even such an educational campaign has its limitations, and pressure from the rank and file of the members may be the controlling factor in determining the policies of the leaders.

Effects on Consumer Supplies

Thus far, the discussion has concerned the effectiveness of the income tax as a means of reducing consumer demand by virtue of its withdrawal of income, its discouragement of spending and its encouragement of demands for higher compensation. There remain to be discussed the effects of the income tax on the supply side, that is, on the amount of goods and services that will be available for purchase.

To the extent that persons are engaged in war production, a decrease in their output may result in either a reduction in war goods and a consequent lengthening of the period of the war or a necessity for shifting more labor to war production from civilian goods production with a consequent decrease in the amount of civilian goods available. To the extent that persons are engaged in production of civilian goods and services, a decrease in their output would be directly reflected in a reduction of the supply of civilian goods and services.

Taxes may decrease production by reducing the standard of living below the point necessary for maximum efficiency, as previously mentioned. They may also decrease production by affecting willingness to work. The effect of an income tax on the willingness of workers to produce would be closely tied in with its effect on the demands for higher compensation. Higher compensation which overcame the effects of the income tax would no doubt also overcome any adverse effect of the tax on their willingness to produce. If the higher compensation were refused, the result might be a slowing up of production and a diminution in output even in the absence of a strike.

A minor indication of the effects of higher taxes on production has been given in recent months by the bracket scale of the withholding tax. The withholding tax is, of course, not the final income tax and any over- or under-withholding is evened out at the end of the year. Nevertheless, there are on record cases of workers who refused to earn additional sums of money in the course of a pay period where the earning of such additional sums would have resulted in application of a higher bracket of withholding and a smaller net wage after withholding. This applies to only small areas of compensation, and as workers come to understand the relation between the amount withheld and the final tax liability the effect should disappear. Nevertheless, it shows that marginal rates of tax are considered by the workers in determining whether they will work more or work less.

In some situations higher taxes may encourage the taxed person to work more hours per week in order to take home the same amount of net earnings after taxes. In such cases higher taxes would have the effect of increasing the supply of labor. High marginal rates of tax may discourage work since the worker may feel that rest and leisure and opportunity to enjoy his income are more important to him than the compensation for additional hours of work after meeting heavy taxes. This would be especially true in the case of overtime work because of the greater exhaustion and loss of leisure accompanying such work. It would also be especially true in the case of a working wife who might find that her earnings after taxes did not compensate her for the additional family costs and the inconvenience accompanying her work outside the home in industry.

Little, if any, evidence has been observed that taxes and rates now imposed or that have been contemplated in programs considered by Congress would actually have a substantial and adverse effect on the willingness to work and on the supply of civilian goods and services.

In the cases of some well-to-do lawyers, professional people, and corporation executives, the high level of income tax rates appears to have caused a diminution of effort, the taking of long vacations, and early retirements. Whether this has been serious during the war, in the face of the strong pressure of patriotism for additional effort, may be questioned. Likewise, the effects of high rates of tax on the taking of risks cannot be ignored. In view of the shortages of manpower and materials, and especially of manpower, it may be that additional willingness to undertake risks in civilian industry would be of little help in increasing civilian supplies during the war period.

Another general effect of the income tax on the supply side relates to the question of general morale. It is not possible to eliminate entirely the equity consideration from the discussion of anti-inflation forces. The willingness of the workers, for example, to give full effort may be impaired if they do not feel that taxes are equitably imposed. Thus, one of the factors in choosing between types of taxes for anti-inflation measures and in determining the rate of an income tax, if that tax is chosen, is whether the resulting distribution of the tax burden will be recognized as an equitable one. The income tax imposed at progressive rates is believed to be recognized generally as the most equitable form of tax.

Workability

An important factor in determining the effectiveness of taxes for the control of inflation is practicability of application. However effective a tax may look on paper, it is of no value if it cannot be practicably applied. The practicability of the individual income tax is as nearly assured as that of any tax. It is true that the recent lowering of exemptions and introduction of current collection raise a question as to workability which has not yet been fully answered. Only after a year or two of operation can it be said positively that the present income tax system is an assured reality for practical use. However, the income tax as revised is already bringing in the money currently, which is the most important factor of workability for inflation control.

Conclusion

The individual income tax proves on examination to be an effective anti-inflation instrument. It has a long history of successful operation, and its administration can effectively carry a very heavy wartime load. Under the present technique of current collection, the timing of the income tax from the standpoint of inflation control is superior to that of most other revenue sources. The income tax does not reach the whole of the national income, but the part it reaches provides an adequate tax base, while the part it does not reach largely represents a necessary minimum which has a strong claim to be shielded on grounds both of equity and of wartime working efficiency. Although it has some indirect inflationary effects in its inducement to wage increases, etc., the individual income tax probably has less effects of this type than any other major tax (with the exception of taxes on estates and perhaps taxes on corporate profit, neither of which can claim the strong anti-inflationary effects of the income tax).

Other taxes can be devised which offer stronger direct incentives to cut spending per dollar raised and which interfere less with the incentives to work long hours, to attract housewives to paying work, etc. But such taxes cannot be applied on a large enough scale to take over much of the load carried by the individual income tax without introducing gross inequities; and these inequities in themselves would undo a good part of the anti-inflationary work of taxation. Accordingly, a substantial strengthening of the individual income tax is an appropriate and effective part of the inflation-control program.

CHAPTER XI

FORCED LOANS

CARL SHOUP

Columbia University

A FORCED LOAN, for purposes of the present discussion, will be restricted to mean only a compulsory contribution of money to the state coupled with a promise of partial or complete repayment with or without interest. The term "forced loan" has also been employed to cover instances where the government forces a supplier of goods or services to accept payment on open account or in obligations that are not legal tender and not receivable in payment of taxes. A still wider extension of the term has applied it to the issuance of paper money, and also to the creation of bank deposits created at the request or command of the government. The present analysis, being concerned with the forced loan chiefly as a wartime device to restrict the total volume of consumer spending, will not make use of these broader meanings.

A forced loan is commonly referred to as "compulsory saving," but this is a misnomer, since the usual forced loan proposal carries no provision that the taxpayer must save to make the loan. He may supply the funds by drawing on his capital or even by going into debt. "Refundable tax" and "postwar credit" are terms that have developed during the present war as synonyms, if not euphemisms, for "forced loan."

An income tax or excess profits tax payment may turn out to have been only a forced loan if a carry-back of losses, or some other averaging of income, results in a tax refund; but the term "refundable tax" is commonly applied only to refunds to which the government is committed in advance.

The Tax Element in a Forced Loan

A forced loan is usually a mixture of tax and voluntary loan. The mixture can be separated by analysis and, under certain circumstances, the two parts can be measured. The attempt to break the forced loan into its constituent parts is worth while, because otherwise the government, in issuing such a loan, may find itself asking much more—or much less—in taxation than it really means to.

The basic difference between a tax and a voluntary loan, relevant for analyzing a forced loan, is that a tax decreases the net worth of the contributor, while a voluntary loan does not. The point is best illustrated by the kind of forced loan that gives the contributor a negotiable certificate. Consider, for instance, a bond bearing no interest. The market value of the bond would be below par until redemption. A valuation of the contributor's assets immediately before and immediately after the forced loan would show an impairment in his economic position. If the current rate of interest for a 10-year bond is, for instance, 2.9 per cent, there is no difference to the individual between (a) paying $25 in tax, and (b) loaning $100 to the government without interest in exchange for a negotiable certificate redeemable at par in 10 years. The forced-loan certificate would have a market value of $75, which is what the individual would have left after paying $25 in tax. In general, any forced loan that carries a rate of interest below the current rate for a similar type of security contains an element of taxation. The size of the tax element is given by the decrease in the net worth of the contributor.

The analysis in terms of decrease in net worth applies even to the contributor who, in the absence of the tax or the forced loan, would not have saved anything. To him, indeed, the important effect of the tax or the forced loan is the involuntary postponement, perhaps permanent reduction,[1] of consumption. But the tax or the forced loan decreases his current consumption by first decreasing his net worth. The distinction drawn above between a tax and a voluntary loan is therefore valid generally, regardless of what any particular taxpayer would do with his money in the absence of either measure.

If the forced-loan certificate is made nonnegotiable, the tax element is not thereby destroyed, but it does become impossible of direct measurement. For example, a certain individual is required to purchase for $100 the non-interest bearing 10-year bond used in the illustration above, except that it is now nonnegotiable, and will not be redeemed until the ten years are up. This individual has no accumulated savings, is spending all his current income, and has a high preference for present over future goods. Suppose that he would voluntarily purchase this kind of a bond only if it were offered to him at $30, that is, he would be willing to cut his current consumption by no more than $30 in order to obtain $100 ten years hence; and if in addition the government were collecting a tax from him of, say, $80, he would be willing to offer no more than $20 for the bond, in view of the larger total decrease in current consumption he would be enduring. Under these circumstances a forced loan of $100 is to him a tax of $80 and a voluntary loan of $20. From

[1] Whether the reduction is permanent depends on how the alternative courses of fiscal policy would affect future price levels.

his point of view the forced loan of $100 leaves him just as he would be if the government taxed him $80 and simultaneously offered him, for voluntary purchase, a $100 certificate (due in 10 years) for $20. In this sense his present net worth is decreased $80 by the forced loan of $100. The fact that the decrease in net worth cannot be measured, because there is no voluntary initial-issue market in such $20 loans, merely means that the government is operating in the dark in imposing taxation on these individuals. This is of course one of the dangers of forced loans on persons with low incomes and no savings; the government may be imposing much more or much less of a tax element on them than it would care to, if it knew the facts.

As the war progressed and this kind of forced loan was repeated, the tax element in it would presumably grow larger. The piling up of these deferred claims by this kind of contributor, who has a strong preference for spending, would, or at least logically should, raise doubts in his mind over the government's ability to hold postwar prices down so that his deferred claims could be satisfied in real terms. Moreover, he would begin to feel the cumulative effects of the decrease in wartime consumption, and the lessening marginal attractiveness of his growing pile of postwar goods.

Continuing with the net-worth approach, it is possible to imagine a case that appears on the surface to be a forced loan, but is in fact purely voluntary. Suppose the forced loan is composed of the same types of negotiable security in the same amounts as would be sold under a voluntary program, although it is distributed differently, everyone being required to purchase an amount corresponding to a uniform percentage of his income. Those of the forced contributors who are involuntary buyers will quickly sell their holdings to those who are not forced to buy as much as they would have purchased voluntarily. The net result is no decrease in the net worth of any of the contributors, hence no tax element in the forced loan.

One more condition is requisite if a tax element is to be present: The government's net worth must increase. This is readily seen in the first example given above. The government receives $100 in cash and incurs an obligation with a present value of only $75. The government also gains in the nonnegotiable-security case, though measurement is impossible. But a forced loan might be so arranged that it decreased the net worth of some contributors while leaving the government with no change in its net worth position. This could happen, it appears, only if the net worth of other government securities increased. The changes would be brought about by internal shifts in the structure of interest rates. Without further analysis this point cannot be considered demonstrated, but something like it might occur if the government were to issue a huge forced loan of medium-term negotiable bonds at the rate of interest prevailing for those bonds before the announcement of the loan. These bonds would presumably fall below par. Since the government would then be offering less of other types of securities during the ensuing year, the market value of some of the other outstanding issues might rise, as the interest-rate structure adapted itself to the changed amount of various types of securities in circulation.

The Chief Purposes of a Forced Loan

In the light of this preliminary analysis, the chief purposes of a forced loan may be considered. A forced loan may be designed to reduce the current level of spending. It may instead be designed merely to lessen the chances that the level of spending will rise; it then aims merely to make the individual's savings more resistant to spending pressure: to increase the average viscosity of savings. An intermediate goal is possible; i.e., to decrease the current pressure on the price control system. Actual spending would not be reduced appreciably, but a less extensive rationing system would be needed, and less policing of prices.

A forced loan designed to reduce the current level of spending must rest in large part on those who have little accumulated savings and who are spending practically all their incomes. For them the forced loan will really mean forced savings. For others the forced loan will presumably result chiefly in a shifting of assets. At least this seems likely for any forced loan expressed as a per cent of income rather than as a per cent of net worth, for reasons to be given below.

To those whose spending will be cut by a forced loan, the loan probably contains a strong tax element. The spending is cut because there is little or no saving to be cut; the lack of saving indicates that present goods are valued highly. The high value put on present goods means that a voluntary loan could not be placed except at an extremely low price, if at all—as for instance in the hypothetical case above where a $100 10-year nonnegotiable bond would be purchased voluntarily only if offered for $30 ($20 if part of a forced loan of $100). The other $70 (or $80) is the tax element in the tax-loan combination. In general, then, a forced loan is likely to reduce the current level of consumption only if it is designed to include a strong element of taxation and a correspondingly weak element of voluntary loan. To these unwilling contributors it is not true that a forced loan postpones, like a voluntary loan, the distribution of the cost of the war. It fixes much of the pattern irrevocably. The $100 that the contributor gets back after the war does not alter this conclusion. This $100 is for him merely the $30 that he surrendered during the war. The other $70 has been taken as part of the distribution of the war costs.

A forced loan designed, not to reduce the current level of spending, but merely to guard against an increase, must on the other hand be directed against those with substantial accumulated savings and a substantial current rate of saving. Those who are already living up to their incomes can be ignored. What the contributors' reactions would be seems practically impossible of prediction. The forced loan would presumably be nonnegotiable and not redeemable before maturity. Might not the contributors react by attempting to get out of some of their other less liquid investments, like mortgages, stocks and bonds with a thin market, equities in land, business buildings and even homes, until the prices of these investments had fallen enough to deter further movement away from them? Contributors already well stocked with such assets might not, therefore, cash in their savings bonds, if any, to meet the forced loan. They would instead be taking measures to maintain their liquidity. For them the forced loan would have an appreciable tax element. But there would be many contributors whose savings were almost entirely in highly liquid form—currency, bank deposits, and savings bonds. It is probably useless to speculate on which form of liquid asset they would surrender. Whichever it was, it seems likely that for them the tax element in the forced loan would not be great; much of these liquid savings are probably so, not because of a strong desire for liquidity, but owing to a lack of knowledge of a safe, less liquid asset. A 3 per cent five-year forced loan (nonmarketable, not redeemable before maturity) might be within a few per cent of being a voluntary loan, with respect to these savings.

On balance, it appears that a forced loan levied as a per cent of current income cannot be counted on to increase the average viscosity of savings by a very substantial percentage. This is especially so if the wartime financing prior to the forced loan has been of a kind to permit of a large accumulation of liquid savings. Even a substantial percentage of one year's surtax net income will then represent only a minor percentage of accumulated liquid savings. And the rate of the forced loan, as a per cent of income, is limited by the fact that it cannot very well exceed the margin left between the existing income tax rate and 100 per cent of the year's income. Otherwise all contributors would have to draw on capital if they were to meet the loan; some contributors would turn out to have no capital (no net worth); allowance would have to be made for net worth position; and the loan would no longer be based solely on income.

At a late stage of war financing that has built up liquid savings, a drastic increase in the viscosity of savings can be accomplished only by a forced loan levied as a per cent of each individual's net worth. Some allowance could be made for the lack of liquidity in the assets held by the contributor before the loan was announced. The apportionment clause in the Federal Constitution raises an interesting legal question for any forced loan of this kind in the United States. The administrative difficulties of a forced loan on a net worth basis would be formidable. And the history of forced-loan proposals in Europe indicates the intense and effective opposition that might be expected from the propertied groups to any forced loan based on net worth rather than income.

The points developed above may be summarized as follows. A forced loan may and commonly does decrease the net worth of the contributor, either as it is measured on the open market, or, if the loan certificates are nonnegotiable, as measured by what he would purchase voluntarily. This decrease in net worth measures the tax element in the forced loan.

A nonnegotiable forced loan levied as a per cent of current income can of course lower the current rate of spending if it is applied to those with low incomes and no substantial savings. For these contributors, however, the forced loan contains a substantial tax element. For them, the difference between such a forced loan and a straight tax of the same amount would not be great. It would probably be much less than is commonly assumed. For those who have accumulated, or are accumulating, savings, this kind of a forced loan serves mainly to increase the average viscosity of their savings rather than to increase the amount of savings, and hinders a rise from the current level of spending. For some of these contributors, already tied up in less liquid investments, the forced loan would carry a strong tax element. For others, floating comfortably on a war-created pool of liquid savings, the forced loan would be almost entirely a voluntary loan. At high income levels the effect even on liquidity would be slight because the rate of the loan would have to be low to stop short of 100 per cent in conjunction with the income tax. A forced loan imposed as a per cent of net worth has much greater possibilities, but is administratively more difficult and might provoke more intense, if narrower, opposition.

Postwar Implications

The postwar implications of a forced loan are not clear. At first sight, the use of a forced loan during the war might seem to offer the government a better opportunity to help achieve economic stability in the postwar period than would be available if voluntary loans or taxes had been used instead—assuming that the terms of the forced loan gave the government considerable latitude in the timing of the repayment. Voluntary loans, it might be argued, would leave the government less control over the total volume of postwar spending if a strong inflationary pressure should develop. Wartime taxation, by the same reasoning, might leave postwar consumers inadequately financed for spending and would put the government under the necessity of deciding how to distribute any purchasing power it might try to inject into the system.

A countervailing consideration, however, is that if any mistake were to occur in the timing of the forced-loan repayment, it could be a very big mistake indeed; ill-advised political pressure or mistaken economic calculations could loose on the market at one time a block of funds large enough to cause substantial damage. Millions of holders of voluntary loans, on the other hand, are not likely to act en masse within a very short period of time. Moreover, it may be doubted whether it would be possible to get acceptance, even in wartime, for a large forced loan—say $20 billion, in the United States, in the present year—if the repayment date were not fixed with some degree of definiteness. In practice, therefore, the forced loan might easily leave the postwar government with less economic maneuverability than the other types of war finance.

On the whole, the postwar considerations must remain undecided, at least until the present gigantic experiment in the creation of liquid assets has run its course. The economist and the student of public finance will face an important research task in the study and interpretation of what happens to these liquid balances when the war is over.

Use of Forced Loans in Present War

Forced loans have a long history, but there is a great difference between the forced loans of the past few years and the forced loans proposed, and occasionally adopted, in earlier periods. The forced-loan proposals that characterized the years immediately after the first World War, and the forced loans of the seventeenth, eighteenth, and nineteenth centuries were designed to obtain funds from those who did not want to lend because they feared default or depreciation, or because they disapproved of the use to which the money would be put. In the present war the forced loan has been used primarily to obtain funds from those who do not want to lend because they prefer to be able to spend.

Use of the forced loan in the present war has been widespread but not intensive. It is significant that after four years of war Great Britain draws a decidedly minor part of her revenue from the forced loan, and that the United States, having neared a peak of wartime spending, has just repealed the small forced-loan element in the individual Victory tax, retaining the forced loan only to the extent of 10 per cent of the corporation excess profits tax. With one very minor exception in the early part of the war, Germany has made no use of the forced loan. Her recent experiment with an induced loan ("iron savings," to be induced by tax relief) seems to have been a failure. Moreover, in both Great Britain and the United States the forced loan was introduced only after tax increases had reached what seemed to be the political ceiling.

Why has the forced loan met with so little favor? Perhaps the answer lies partly in a preference for direct controls (price control and rationing) applied at specific points, as compared with general measures to restrict spending by decreasing disposable income, and partly in less concern, with respect to the postwar period, over the piling up of liquid assets than over the accumulation of a public debt outside the banking system. If the experience of Germany and Italy after the last war is a guide, the forced loan on a large scale will attract attention in more than one country as an alternative to a capital levy in the postwar period.

CHAPTER XII

SOCIAL SECURITY TAXES AND INFLATION

Seymour E. Harris

Harvard University

In 1935 the United States Government introduced a social security program which, *inter alia*, provided for old age and unemployment insurance. The rate of taxation under the unemployment insurance program was to be 3 per cent for employers and the states might levy additional taxes on employees. Under federal old age and survivors insurance, the program called for a rate of taxation of 1 per cent on employers and 1 per cent on employees, the rate to be gradually increased until the maximum of 3 per cent for each group was reached. The rate under the latter program has remained at 2 per cent in all as the result of later legislation by Congress. Recently Congress voted to continue the 2 per cent rate for this year in any case. Under unemployment insurance very few states have imposed taxes on employees as well as employers.

Potential Rise of Payroll Taxes

There can be little doubt but that the government has failed to make the maximum use of payroll taxes in the fight against inflation. For example, in the period of June 30, 1940, to November, 1943, the national debt rose approximately $122 billion. Of this total, special issues which are absorbed by various insurance and pension programs accounted for only $7.5 billion or roughly 6 per cent.

The possibilities are evidenced from the following. Let us suppose that the original plan of a 6 per cent tax equally paid by employers and employees for old age insurance had been carried through by 1941 and also that unemployment insurance taxes had been doubled, namely an increase from 3 to 6 per cent, the increase being shared equally by employees and employers. (The Wagner bill requires a 5 per cent additional tax on employees and 2 per cent on employers.) In that case, assuming that the war will continue through 1946, the increase of payroll taxes would have been approximately $9 billion for the years 1941 to 1943 and $13 billion for the years 1944 to 1946, or a net gain of $22 billion. These are, of course, necessarily rough estimates being based on past, current, and future covered payrolls.

Most arguments adduced in support of forced loans may be used in support of higher payroll taxes. Employees are promised repayment of both capital and interest in a later period, not only of their contributions but also those of their employers. Increased payroll taxes are especially effective as anti-inflationary weapons since the burden is put upon those who consume a very large part of their income. Workers will be forced to cut consumption almost as much as their taxes are increased and their wages are reduced following the imposition of taxes on employees.

If it were administratively possible, it would be desirable to exempt from the proposed *increases* workers with low incomes (say $1,500 for a family). To that extent, the yield would be lower than is here indicated.

This potential contribution of $22 billion over 6 years of war or almost $5 billion annually at the peak might have been a material factor in the fight against inflation. Compare the annual gains with the amount of inflationary borrowing, that is, loans to the government by banks or out of balances that otherwise would have been idle. This inflationary borrowing in the years of intense war activity is of the order of $20 billion annually. A contribution of $4-5 billion annually in the years 1944-1946 out of payroll taxes will absorb perhaps 25 per cent of this excess. The gains, however, might be much larger because the imposition of heavier taxes on payrolls would make it much easier to increase taxes all around. For example, the imposition of several billion dollars of additional taxes on payrolls might make it possible to impose an additional tax program of $10 billion per year. A good deal of the opposition to further increases in income and corporate taxation and also excise taxes on luxuries rests in part upon the failure to impose heavier taxes on the aristocracy of labor largely covered by the social security program. It should be observed, furthermore, that taxation of payrolls is much to be preferred to sales taxation. In the first place, the employees covered under payroll programs are on the whole the better paid employees; and secondly, the taxation rests on those who have jobs as against sales taxes which rest both on those who do not have jobs and also on those who do not have adequate purchasing power.

Some Gains From Higher Payroll Taxes

This program also has the advantage of a transfer of purchasing power in a period when supplies are scarce to a period when they are more likely to be plentiful. What the government proposes to do in this case is to remove purchasing power in the hands of those who are likely to spend, and to pass on that purchasing power to the same groups or their survivors in later periods when goods will be more plentiful. In that way, those who are employed now and who are relatively young will give up part of their goods, which in any case they would have to give up largely through other measures (e.g., inflation and other forms of taxation), and receive in return additional supplies when they are unemployed or when they are older.

It is also of importance that the lower income groups spend a larger part of their income and are subject to less personal taxation than the higher income groups. Thus, according to a recent study, income and corporate taxes in the United States are up from $3.4 billion to $35.8 billion or ninefold from 1940 to 1944; but all taxes are up only 2½ times or from $14.4 billion to $50.6 billion.[1] Under the personal income tax for 1943 the payments for those with net *income* before exemptions are:

Income	*Tax*
$ 1,000	$ 107
2,000	345
10,000	2,973
100,000	70,516

Lower income groups can stand more taxation; and this type of taxation is very effective in cutting consumption. For example, in 1942 income groups earning less than $3,000 accounted for 42 per cent of money income, only 6 per cent of the direct taxes, and 52 per cent of total consumption.[2] Payrolls have increased from $44 billion in 1939 to more than $100 billion in 1943. Nevertheless, there has been no increase in the rate of taxation for social security and, moreover, the percentage of social security taxes to national income has remained roughly unchanged, whereas the percentage of taxation to national income from 1939-40 to 1943-

---

[1] R. A. Musgrave, "The Wartime Tax Effort in the United States, the United Kingdom, and Canada," *Federal Reserve Bulletin*, XXX (January, 1944), 24.

[2] OPA study on *Civilian Spending and Saving, 1941 and 1942*, p. 4. This is for the year 1942.

44 has risen from 19 to 32 per cent. In 1940-41, the payroll taxes inclusive of unemployment insurance accounted for $1,930 million and in 1942-43, $2,815 million. The ratio to national income payments was 2.3 per cent and 2.1 per cent respectively.

Arguments Against Higher Payroll Taxes

Before turning to the reasons for the failure to step-up rates, I should like to say a word concerning unemployment insurance because the arguments that follow apply to old-age insurance. A rise of rates is especially replete with difficulties in unemployment insurance despite the fact that one-third of receipts received up to date have been spent as compared with only 10 per cent for old age insurance. Accumulation of large balances for the former brings pressure for reduction of rates or liberalization of benefits. The argument for a further increase in rates now is that the great burden of postwar liberalization of social security may in part be put upon the taxpayer now because he can carry it more easily at the present time than in any period of unemployment later. The other alternative is a rise of public debt later.

One may ask, why has there not been an increase in payroll taxes for old age insurance? Many explanations may be offered.

A generally accepted fallacy, which has been widely disseminated by Senator Vandenberg, John Flynn, and others first requires our attention. The argument is that social security reserves invested in public securities amount, according to rather extreme statements, to a swindle. Reserves invested in debt is a sham according to these authorities. Wide acceptance of this position played no small part in the revision of the social security program in 1939; but it has little substance. It is perhaps true that in peacetimes the provision of a guaranteed market for government securities offered by the inflow of dollars in social security reserves might to some extent increase expenditures, and in so far as that is true the effect may very well be an increase of public debt. If the debt became too large, then repudiation of obligations either directly or through inflation was feared by some. In so far as the debt burden grows rapidly, there may be some question raised as to whether the social security payments will be paid in stable dollars. Even in peacetime there is little in this line of argument. In so far as the social security reserves hold a large volume of public securities, a smaller volume is held elsewhere. And expenditures only to a small extent will be determined by the provision of this additional market for government securities. In wartime, moreover, expenditures have very little to do with the provision of a market for government securities through social security payments. Expenditures are determined primarily by military and political considerations. Neither in peacc nor war, finally, is there a better investment for social security reserves than government issues.

There is another argument that has much more truth in it, namely, that social security must be paid for by the generations who are living when the payments are being made. In other words, social security payments represent a drain on the goods and services available in any given period. It follows from this, according to many, that we should pursue a pay-as-go plan and not bother to collect payroll taxes or to build up a reserve. This position is substantially correct. Yet it must be pointed out that the method of financing social security will play an important part in the determination of the tax burden on future generations and the income potential of future generations. If too large a part of the tax burden for social security is placed upon future generations, then the excessive tax burden in 19XX will have an adverse effect on the current output of goods in the year 19XX. In that sense, the method of financing social security plays an important part in the determination of the national income, the tax potential and hence the benefit structure of social security. How many of us know that we are accumulating billions of dollars of social security obligations in later years against which small provision is being made? By 1960, this obligation will probably be several billion dollars per year and by 1980 even more. It is strange indeed that those who oppose the growth of public debt have played such a large part in the accumulation of debt on social security account. The present value of future obligations is much greater than the amounts that have been provided to meet them.

Another and related argument is that when the time comes to make large social security payments productivity will be much higher and, therefore, it will be much easier to levy the necessary taxes in, say, 1960 or 1980 than in 1945. This argument also should carry weight. It should be pointed out, however, that although our average productivity per year has increased at the rate of 3 per cent per year for 50 years, it does not follow that progress will continue at the same rate. Assuming, however, that it will, it still remains true that in 1960 or 1980 additional tax burdens will be put upon the federal treasury. We can already envisage very large expenditures for military purposes, veterans, public investment, and other social services.

The Deflationary Argument

Another argument that was made much of in the decision to refrain from stepping up social security taxes has been that the taxes are deflationary. Undoubtedly, the accumulation of reserves in 1936-37 did to some extent cause an absorption of purchasing power and contributed towards the deflation of the 1937-38 period. There are, however, other explanations of the downward trend that occurred in that period, and the excess of receipts over expenditures or the reduction of the excess of expenditures by government is only one part of the explanation.[3]

Many have argued against a stepping up of social security taxes in the war period because although they see the advantage in terms of the anti-inflationary pressure, they are fearful that an increase in the rate of taxation on payrolls in the war period will be an excuse for the maintenance of these high rates in the postwar period when they are no longer necessary. I see much weight in this position, especially since I am one of those economists who believe that one of the difficult problems of the postwar period is to maintain consumption and investment at a sufficiently high level to assure employment, and also believe that there are institutional factors which in a period of high income or rising income tend to prevent the income above a given level from being fully spent. High payroll taxes may, therefore, have an unfortunate effect on the economic situation. I, nevertheless, hold that we ought to prepare for any such discouragement of consumption in the postwar period by the provision of administrative discretion in the reduction of payroll taxes when given indices of employment and income reveal that such a reduction is necessary. For example, when unemployment rises above a certain level, or national income falls below a certain level, then payroll taxes should be reduced for the next three months by a given percentage. This delegation of the taxing

[3] These explanations are discussed more fully in *Economics of Social Security*, by S. E. Harris. They are not relevant for the present problem.

power does not seem greater than that under the Reciprocal Trade Agreements.

Finance Through General Taxation

Another and related point used by many who oppose an increase in payroll taxes is that the financing of social security should largely be put upon general taxes and not upon those who receive benefits. This position has been taken in the Beveridge Report and it has been taken in the National Resources Planning Board report on *Security, Work and Relief Policies*. Here the emphasis is put not alone upon the relationship to employment or the demand for consumption and investment goods, but also on grounds of justice. They contend that those who can afford to pay should do so, and those who cannot afford to pay should not. Social security is then a means of redistributing income so that everyone is guaranteed a minimum standard of living. This argument and the preceding one are, of course, of some importance and should be given due weight. These are long-run considerations and should not carry much weight in the present situation. We should have an appraisal of our social security program for the postwar period, and we should decide whether the burden should be put upon those who benefit, or upon the taxpayer in general. I am sympathetic with these latter contentions, but nevertheless I am also impressed by the importance of the anti-inflationary fight which will concern future generations and by the need of not putting too heavy a burden of taxation on future generations. In the area of long-run policy I am, moreover, influenced by the argument that those who profit from social security should pay in so far as they have capacity to pay. This is not only in order to make them feel that it is their program, but it is also to protect them against failure of later Congresses to appropriate the necessary sums of money.

Can the Burden Be Put Upon Labor?

Many have objected to an increase of payroll taxes on the ground that recourse to heavy taxes, particularly on labor, results in their being passed onto the consumer in higher prices. In other words, the entrepreneur, under present circumstances, will assume that an increase in the payroll tax is an increase of costs and he will pass on the tax in higher prices. In so far as the employee is asked to pay the tax, he demands higher wages and the result again is a rise of prices. The problem of the incidence of payroll taxes is a very complicated one, and I have devoted a couple of hundred pages in my book on social security to that problem. I still believe that for the most part wages are determined by marginal productivity and that employers who are asked to absorb a tax for labor will try to pass that tax on to labor or to consumers in higher prices. But at the present time they will find some difficulty in passing taxes on in higher prices of commodities. This follows because there is control of prices. Yet one cannot deny the general argument that in the state of the present labor market, the pressure to pass on payroll taxes asssessed on employees will be strong and may have a considerable success. In so far as this is true, the effect will be a reduction of profits or a rise of prices. Since profits of corporations prior to payment of taxes have gone up from $5 to $23 billion from 1939 to 1943, there is plenty of room for absorption on the part of the entrepreneur. Nevertheless, in the present state of price control which is not tight, entrepreneurs may be able to pass a considerable proportion of their payroll taxes, both their own and their employees, on in the form of higher prices. I conclude that in the present war situation the general argument that payroll taxes, whether assessed on employers or employees, are paid by the workers does not carry as much weight as usual, and to that extent an increase in payroll taxes will not have as great an anti-inflationary effect as it otherwise might. In part, the consumer will pay; and in part, both employers and employees will bear the ultimate burden through a reduction of rewards and higher prices of purchases.

Payroll Taxation: Its Contribution to Anti-Inflation

I conclude with a few comments on the general inflationary picture. Too much, of course, cannot be expected from an increase of taxation in general, nor from an increase in payroll taxes. National income will undoubtedly rise to $160 billion or more. There should not be much more than $90 billion of consumption goods available. The excess of income over supplies of consumption goods available will be $70 billion. These are of course guesses, and the estimates of consumption in particular may prove to be wrong as earlier ones have. Perhaps $25 billion of these $70 billion will be taken away in direct personal taxes, leaving $45 billion more to be absorbed. If the government can absorb a large part of the remaining $45 billion through the sale of government securities, then the inflationary danger will not be great. Unfortunately, it is not likely that the government will be entirely successful. My guess is that there still will be an excess of $20 billion which will be a serious threat to the effectiveness of price control and rationing. If social security taxation accounts for $4 billion or $5 billion of additional taxation, then to that extent the inflationary pressures to violate price regulations resulting from excesses of money will be reduced. In this manner, part of the excess purchasing power will be sterilized. Too much should not, however, be expected from this rise in payroll taxes because in part the gains will be reduced through the passing on of the taxes in higher prices and to some extent the gains will be lost through a reduction in voluntary lending. Any tax program, or any compulsory loan program, is bound to have repercussions in terms of the effect on other means of getting cash. The government gets more through loans if it gets less through taxes; and if it gets more through taxes, it gets less through loans. In particular, the increase of labor costs associated with higher payroll taxes will result in a reduction in the yield of excess profits taxes.

The Public Debt and Reserves

A final word on the public debt and social security reserves. When the war ends the public debt may well be $300 billion. The following figures are of some interest.[4]

Date	*Public Debt*	*Special Issues*
June, 1940	$ 42.4 billion	$ 4.8 billion
June, 1943	135.4	10.9
June, 1946	285.0 (Estimated by Author)	18.0 (Estimated)

We might have had (assuming the war continues until 1946) $40 billion of public debt in various social security and insurance reserves. (This is subject to the reservations in the last section and allowances for any minimum exemptions for the increase of rates.) Our future tax burden would to that extent have been greater in war when we could afford it and when it would do the most good, and less after the war.

The public debt of $285 billion can be financed without inflation or devastating deflation, and the social security re-

---

[4] *Bulletin of Treasury Department,* December, 1943, p. 59.

serves then will not be dissipated through inflation or through serious declines of national income following deflation. I am impressed by the fact that our industrial potential, with $20 billion of new plant, tremendous improvements in technology and administration, 16 millions of additional workers, with vast gains in agriculture and mining, is greater than ever. We started the war with $300 billion or more of wealth. Who will say that if the debt should grow by $300 billion, the country is worth nothing? And who will not say that with an income potential of $100-150 billion in 1940 prices we are not vastly richer than ever before? The $300 billion of debt is an annoyance and involves transfers and taxation. If we attain anything near our potential we shall be left with a national income, after payment of public debt interest and repayment in good times, much beyond what we have ever had before in peacetime.

Summary

In summary, we might have had $22 billion more in payroll taxes in the years 1941-46, and we may still save part of this sum. Large amounts of additional revenue might still be had through an increase of payroll taxes from 5 per cent to 12 per cent. The contributions would be larger if allowance is made for the effects on other tax rates. Heavier taxes now would reduce inflationary burdens and be assessed when the burden can most easily be endured, with the promise of relief if necessary in the postwar. It is also pointed out that low income groups could stand heavier taxation.

We also deal with the long-run arguments against the accumulation of reserves and indicate the extent to which they may be accepted, and the deflationary aspects both prewar and postwar. Clearly any social security and tax policies should be reviewed in the postwar period when an entirely different tax structure is wanted. It is admitted also that the anti-inflationary effects are reduced in so far as the taxes are offset through higher prices and higher wages.

Finally we have commented on the weight of the postwar debt in which the reserves will be invested.

PART FOUR

EXPERIENCE OF OTHER COUNTRIES IN CURBING INFLATION THROUGH FISCAL DEVICES

CHAPTER XIII

CONTROLLING INFLATION IN THE U.S.S.R.

ARTHUR Z. ARNOLD

New York University

INFLATION IN THE TWENTIES

THE PEOPLE and the government of the Soviet Union still remember that twenty years ago, when the volume of money in circulation in their country exceeded 800 quadrillion rubles, the old currency was redeemed at the rate of 50 billion rubles for one new treasury ruble. The price index on March 1, 1924, (1913 = 100) stood at about 16 trillion.[1] The borrowing and lending of credit, the production of commodities, their sale and purchase, and all other transactions encountered in a modern economy took on a purely speculative character.

No one knew the extent to which the purchasing power of a sum of money loaned today would shrink thirty days hence, and, therefore, what interest rate to charge for the loan. The producer and the trader could not know what price would enable them to replace their stock and earn a profit. Wages, even if increased in the morning to a point which would insure a standard of health and decency, paid and spent later *in the same day* brought a lowered standard of living. Financial planning was impossible. Cost accounting

---

[1] Arthur Z. Arnold, *Banks, Credit and Money in Soviet Russia,* pp. 186-87, 224 ff.

was quite meaningless. Bookkeeping itself became exceedingly involved.

The problem of how to get rid of paper money (sovznaks) as soon as it was received was considered more important than cost calculation. An hour's difference in the purchase or deposit of the relatively more stable money—banknotes (chervontzy)—meant a gain or a loss as high as five per cent or even more. Speculation in currency became nation-wide. Estimates of government receipts and expenditures were of little help. The lag between the collection of revenue in a currency that was depreciating fast and its expenditure meant an appreciable loss to the treasury.

Bringing Inflation Under Control

The Monetary Reform of 1924 constituted a great achievement; it saved the country from a hyper-inflationary morass which threatened to swallow it. The economic life of the country began to assume normal aspects. Industry, which in 1920 accounted for less than 20 per cent of the prewar output, continued to expand and in 1928 almost attained the 1913 level.

The introduction of the first Five-Year Plan in 1928 called for a very rapid industrialization of the country. Particular stress was being laid on "heavy" industry and the production of means of production. All of which called for capital funds of gigantic proportions.

Since the country had no capital accumulation and since the outside world was to have no part in its industrial expansion, it became necessary to restrict the production of consumers' goods. Capital accumulation on a large scale was made possible by the "tightening of the consumer's belt."

The second Five-Year Plan (1933-37) called for further rapid industrialization. It did provide for a considerable expansion of the output of consumers' goods, but the threat of war with Japan and Germany caused the Soviet Union to lay greater stress on military preparations and the development of strategic industries in the Urals and the east in general.

Under the third Five-Year Plan industrial production in 1942 was to have exceeded that in 1937 by almost 90 per cent, while general agricultural production in 1942 was to have topped that in 1937 by 50 per cent.[2] The consumer's plane of living would have been considerably improved. In fact, toward the completion of the second Five-Year Plan and following the opening of the third Five-Year Plan the flow of manufactured consumers' goods into the market became appreciably increased. War preparations and then the outbreak of the war put a stop to all of this.

Under a free competitive system a disparity between the output of capital goods and consumers' goods such as existed in the Soviet Union would send prices skyrocketing. The ruble, however, lived a sheltered life in a *planned economy* amidst a regime of extreme centralization of authority.

Rationing

As early as 1928-29 the government introduced ration cards entitling the holders to buy at so-called *closed* shops or stores limited quantities of goods at relatively low prices. But already by 1930 the prices of a number of commodities in the "private" sector exceeded those in the "socialized" sector by from 12 to 15 times.[3] Prices in the *closed* shops kept on moving to higher levels. In 1933 the government began to

---

[2] Eugene Varga, *Two Systems: Socialist Economy and Capitalist Economy*, p. 240.

[3] G. Neiman, "Abolition of Ration Cards," *Problemy Ekonomiki*, 1935, No. 1, p. 49. Quoted in Arnold, *op. cit.* p. 424.

open so-called *commercial* shops or stores at which anybody could buy goods in any quantity but at considerably higher prices than at the *closed* shops. During the first quarter of 1934 prices (in rubles) per kilogram (2.2 pounds) were approximately as follows:[4]

Commodity	*Closed Shop*	*Commercial Shop*
Black bread	0.54 rubles	2.00 rubles
White bread	1.04	3.00
Meat	2.00-4.00	10.00-12.00
Butter	6.00-8.00	30.00

It should be understood that the Soviet Union discontinued the publication of price indexes in 1931.

The progress made by the national economy in general, the improved technique and organization in agriculture, as well as the legalization in 1933 of markets in which "collective farmers" were allowed to sell their surplus foodstuffs paved the way for the abolition of the rationing cards. By the end of 1935 the rationing system and its "closed" shops became largely a thing of the past. A month or so later the "Torgsin" system of stores, where goods of a rather wide variety and good quality were sold for precious metals and foreign currency (transmitted, e.g., by relatives in the United States), terminated their existence. Henceforth, all living in a given region whether workers, priests, officials, or teachers were to pay the same prices for commodities with no restrictions as to the quantity purchased. Prices, however, were fixed approximately midway between the ration prices and those which were charged by "commercial" shops. But, as has been said before, the volume of consumers' goods kept on rising.

The shift to war production was responsible for the reintroduction of the rationing system.

---

[4] Erich Wollengerg, "The Abolition of Bread Cards in the Soviet Union," *The New International*, a Monthly Organ of Revolutionary Marxism (New York), March, 1935, 11, No. 2, 73-74. Quoted in Arnold, *op. cit.*, p. 425.

Price Rises

The Soviet Union at present is confining the production of consumers' goods to a barest minimum—a minimum hardly imaginable in the United States. What then of the purchasing power of the ruble in a war economy of this type?

The prices prevailing in the government stores in the first half of 1943 in rubles per kilogram were as follows:[5]

Bread	2.70	rubles
Meat	12.80	"
Butter	24.50	"
Cheese	16.00	"
Potatoes	0.65	"

As has already been pointed out there exist in Soviet cities "open markets" in which prices are free to rise to any height. In these markets farmers sell for cash or exchange for bread or manufactured goods, milk, vegetables, berries and meat. Collective farmers are allowed to cultivate small patches of land on their own account and to dispose of the produce as they choose. At present, however, due to the shortage of manufactured goods, the farmers prefer to consume the greater part of their produce.

In these "open markets" the prices in rubles per kilogram are:

Bread	100	rubles
Meat	350	"
Butter	700	"
Cheese	500	"
Potatoes	60	"

Good secondhand suits, are from 8,000 to 10,000 rubles. In general, the prices charged in the "open markets" are from 20 to 100 times higher than those in the state shops. The

[5] The current data and information used here are based upon material gathered by a competent and reliable foreigner in the Soviet Union. To repeat, the Soviet Union does not publish price indexes. It is difficult for a private individual to determine to what extent the sample gathered by him is representative.

"open markets," however, handle no more than one to two per cent of the total volume of consumers' goods produced.

The prices in the open markets, which before the war were something like three to four times those in the stores, reached their height by the end of 1941. *Since then they have remained stable.*

The low-grade urban manual factory worker of ordinary ability (i.e., one who has not managed to increase his output above the average or in other words one who is not a "Stakhanovite"), whose monthly wage is 400 rubles, cannot make purchases in these markets. But "Stakhanovites" earn as high as 3,000-4,000 rubles monthly, and managers and technicians can earn even more. In the state shops, the "closed" shops, they can buy no more than that to which their rations entitle them.

Wartime Anti-Inflation Controls

The wartime anti-inflation controls in the Soviet Union do not differ much from the controls which were in operation prior to the shift to a total war economy.

The Soviet economy is a planned economy in which all units are coordinated under a central authority and operate according to plan. Industry, with minor exceptions, is state owned. The state stores, the "closed" shops, are state owned. The state plans the output of consumers' goods and fixes the rations, and prices. The state plans the total payroll. Once it is known what is to be paid out in wages and what will be collected in taxes, railroad fare, subscriptions to war loans etc., it is relatively easy to determine the purchasing power in the hands of the people. An increase in the rates of taxation, war loan subscriptions, prices, etc., will mop up the surplus purchasing power.

Under these circumstances prices in retail establishments

where goods are rationed cannot possibly rise, if the state does not wish them to rise, no matter what the volume of paper money in circulation happens to be.

But fraud, pilferage and graft cannot be ruled out even in a planned economy. The sales people by short-weighing, or by falsifying the records, may be able to appropriate some of the goods and sell them privately (a sort of "black" market) or in the legalized "open markets."

To fight these tendencies rigid control was introduced with respect to inventories and accounting practices. Thus, the People's Commissariat of Trade announced that beginning with March 1, 1943, inventories would be taken every month at unspecified dates in stores and every three months in warehouses and supply centers. It set up a Chief Administration of State Trade Inspection with agencies throughout the country. Furthermore, the State Committee of Defense charged the trade unions with the duties of supervising trading and public feeding establishments. They are to inspect the weights and measures, to see that goods intended for holders of ration cards reach them, that the fixed rations and prices are not violated, and that reasonable sanitary conditions are maintained. Trade unions elect from among their members the "public controllers" who are doing the actual supervising required of the unions. The workers perform this work in their spare time, but are excused from certain compulsory overtime duties at the factories. Thus, the control is from above (the state) and from below (the consumer, the worker).

Fiscal Controls

Among the fiscal controls—and these on the whole are not new in the Soviet Union—the following may be mentioned: income tax; direct war tax; and finally, state loans. The "turnover" (sales) tax used to play a very important role in the Soviet Union.

In its attempt to raise the productivity of labor to considerably higher levels than those which prevailed in the country, the government encouraged workers to follow the example of a worker named Stakhanov who succeeded in speeding-up production to a very high level. The offer of high incomes appealed to the workers. The shortage of consumers' goods necessitated the employment of the device of direct income taxation. It may be said, of course, that "Stakhanovism" (i.e., the movement to speed up production) led to the development of differences in income levels and that this in turn led to the extension of direct income taxes. It may be that to some extent this is true. It must be remembered, however, that the distribution of incomes is a part of the plan and that the Soviet economy does not have to resort to taxation in order to redistribute incomes. The government does not wish to destroy the incentives which are instrumental in raising the productivity of labor.

A worker earning 150 rubles per month pays somewhat in excess of three per cent in income taxes. The highest tax—13 per cent—is paid by those whose monthly wages or salaries exceed 1,000 rubles.

In addition to the above tax, workers and employees pay what is known as a *war tax* amounting to 10 per cent of one's income—easy to compute.

Writers, artists, singers, etc., whose incomes are not determined directly by the state, pay taxes on that part of their incomes which does not exceed 12,000 rubles a year at a rate approximately the same as workers and employees, but as the income increases the rate goes up until it rises to 55 per cent on incomes in excess of 300,000 rubles per year. Professional men and women in *private* practice are required to pay rates that are approximately double those for workers and employees; these rates rise to 55 per cent on incomes in excess of 70,000 rubles. Artisans, who prefer not to join co-operatives, pay even higher rates. It will be observed that taxation of these groups—except in the case of writers, artists, etc.—is not merely to serve the purpose of raising revenue or removing excess purchasing power. It is also intended to stimulate cooperative effort.

Subscription to the war loans is supposed to be voluntary but in reality workers are expected to subscribe to the extent of about one month's wages. The First State War Loan in 1942 sought to raise 10 billion rubles, but within a few days the state succeeded in raising 13.2 billion rubles. The Second State War Loan drive was launched during the first week of June, 1943. Its aim was to raise 12 billion rubles, and again within a few days the loan was oversubscribed reaching 20,323,032,000 rubles—a sum constituting approximately 10 per cent of the estimated national money income.

The war loans constitute an excellent device for removing excess purchasing power. For example, the farmers' cash incomes nowadays are rather exceptionally high and so their quotas for the war loans were fixed very high. Incidentally, they oversubscribed those quotas. It may also be added that this caused them to sell more of their produce in the open markets.

It must not be forgotten that the plan enables the government to remove excess purchasing power from the agricultural sector by means of other devices as well.

The plan, for example, may require the collectives to set aside a considerable portion of their earnings for capital improvements, etc.[6] Too, all farms (even independent) must

[6] Before the war 90 per cent of the sown area was organized as "collective" farms; about 8 per cent as "state" farms (like factories); and about 2 per cent of the sown area was cultivated by individual peasants.

deliver to the state a part of the produce at a *fixed* price (independents had to deliver a larger percentage at such prices—it did not pay to remain an "independent"). It is, however, the state which fixes such prices. Moreover, the farmers pay in kind for the use of tractors. The tractors cannot be privately owned. The state fixes prices at which farmers buy manufactured goods in stores operated for their benefit.

The Soviet Union on the whole has been relatively successful in its attempts to keep inflationary pressures within control. The termination of the war will of course lead to an expansion of the volume of consumers' goods. But the problem of reconstruction, rebuilding the devastated areas, will be a most serious one. It will not throw the Soviet Union, as some people think, into the position where it was in the early twenties. The Soviet Union will not start from absolute scratch. It has accumulated much experience and has, so to speak, the blueprints. Its planning system operates in such a way as to prevent a repetition of an inflation of the kind that plagued the country in the twenties.

CHAPTER XIV

ITALY'S EXPERIENCE IN CURBING INFLATION THROUGH FISCAL DEVICES*

GEORGE A. TESORO

The American University; former Editor-in-chief of the Rivista Italiana di Diritto Finanziario

INTRODUCTION

THE PRESENT study deals with the fiscal devices used by the Italian Fascist government to control inflation from 1935 to July 25, 1943, when Mussolini's overthrow occurred. Later developments belong to an entirely new and different stage, which cannot be considered here, owing in part to the paucity of the available information, but above all to the present fluid and chaotic state of conditions in the Italian peninsula.[1]

In discussing Fascist inflation-control measures, it is desirable to consider separately two periods. The first covers the period of the wars in Abyssinia, Spain, and Albania, and of the feverish (though ultimately inept) preparations for the world war that was expected. The second deals with the years of World War II.

---

* Grateful acknowledgement is made to the Rockefeller Foundation, whose grant allowed the author to carry on extensive research on Italian war finance. The present paper is based mainly on data gathered for the broader inquiry conducted as a result of the grant.

1 Existing literature on Italian war finance includes only two studies: B. G. Foa and P. G. Treves, "Italian Finance and Investment," in *Economica*, August, 1939, and Lanfrancus, "La politica finanziaria del governo fascista (1936-1941)" in *Quaderni Italiani*, Boston, Mass., January, 1942.

During the first period, the problem of inflation control did not present formidable or unmanageable difficulties for various reasons. The national economy and income had recovered from the depths of the 1932-1933 period, but were still well below the full employment level. There were certain employment bottlenecks and a certain amount of profit inflation. Domestic prices were rising far in excess of world prices owing to the rationing of imports, the high cost of "autarchic" production, and a growing preference of the public for "stable value" investments. But there were still widespread areas of depression and unemployment.

Hence, the chief problem of this period was not to check an outright inflationary spiral, but to devote an increasingly large share of the modest Italian real income to war and to autarchic production by financing the various military adventures of the Fascist government in such a way as to avoid a more rapid expansion of money income than that of the income-earning activity in Italy. In other words, the problem was one of "pre-inflation" control.

At that time, the Fascist machinery of economic controls was still pretty tight and effective. After his cheap victory over Abyssinia and, by implication, over the League of Nations powers, Mussolini found himself surrounded for a year or two with a halo of success, which facilitated the execution of his domestic policies. Moreover, he made full use of the skillful advice of Italian experts of the pre-Fascist era, and of competent officials in the Italian ministry of finance.

The moderate proportions of the problem and the favorable general atmosphere permitted the fascist regime to keep the economic and financial situation fairly well in hand up to the summer of 1940. Mussolini's intervention in World War II, against the almost unanimous will and wishes of the Italian people, created an altogether different situation, and eventually brought about its nemesis—in financial no less than political and general affairs.

What happened in Italy—soon after the brief summer of easy successes and high expectations of quick victory was over—was that the country went gradually on a "sit-down" strike. By various stages, the government lost control of the situation. As before the war, it could legislate at will without the slightest popular or other control. But the enforcement machinery broke down because the people did not cooperate, because of corruption and inefficiency, and because the magnitude of the problems was such as to become almost unmanageable.

The delivery of farm products to warehouses (compulsory by law, and extended on paper to practically all crops) steadily decreased. The rationing system became ineffective, and black markets and all types of private barter developed and prospered. The subsidy system swallowed ever-growing amounts of funds. The financial strain became more and more intolerable.

The deterioration was continuous, and very serious, throughout the first two years of the war. In the fall of 1942, with the beginning of mass air raids against the Italian cities, and with the prospects of victory finally destroyed by Stalingrad and by the landing in North Africa, the situation in Italy—which until then, though bad, had been kept somehow under control—became almost chaotic. The mass evacuations from the city disturbed whatever was left of normal economy, imposed a heavy burden on transportation and all other available facilities, and involved heavy disbursements from the Treasury. In addition, these exoduses brought about an enormously enlarged demand for bank notes and liquid currency. This obviously widened the already large inflationary gap.

To form an approximate idea of the inflationary process which was under way in Italy between 1935 and 1943, we should consider the total purchasing power available for disposal by the Italian people and the total supply of goods and services available for civilian consumption.

Italy's national monetary income was swollen by the government's extraordinary war (and related) expenditures: from 1934-35 through 1939-40, 67.0 billion lire; in 1940-41, 57.7; in 1941-42, 71.3; in 1942-43, 81.0 billion. We should add to these figures the ordinary expenditures of the Italian government, which gradually increased from 20.8 billion lire in 1934-35 to 54.1 billion lire in 1942-43 (including the increased burden of interest caused by war borrowing). We then have a fair indication of the enormous financial burden placed on the Italian people by the Fascist regime, and of the order of magnitude of the inevitable increase in the monetary income, i.e., in the existing purchasing power.[2]

On the other hand, the amount of goods and services available for the civilian population gradually decreased during the period considered, because of the overexpanding utilization of productive facilities (including manpower) for military purposes, and, after 1942, because of the economic disruption caused by the war, especially by air bombing. In the light of these considerations we may understand the size of the widening inflationary gap which the Fascist regime had to face during its aggressive adventures.

---

[2] Accurate estimates of the Italian national income during the last few years are not available. In 1935, it was estimated at 80 billion lire. For 1943, the highest available estimate is 170 billion. (See *Frankfurter Zeitung*, July 18, 1943.) This, however, seems too low in relation to total state expenditures of 135 billion lire in the fiscal year 1942-43. If we estimate the 1942-43 national income at 230 billion lire, the part available for private consumption (after deduction of all central government expenditures) amounted in that fiscal year to 95 billion. Because of the increase in prices, however, this corresponded roughly to only 40 per cent of the amount of goods and services available for private consumption in 1938-39.

The central objective of Italy's war finance, and of its attempts to curb inflation, has always been the skimming off of surplus purchasing power through government borrowing. Since part of the borrowing was compulsory, the fiscal devices used in Italian war finance included both taxes and compulsory loans. An original scheme of "privileged saving," although announced and widely advertised in 1942, was never realized.[3]

Taxes on Income

In the fiscal year 1942-43 direct taxes represented 29 per cent of the ordinary revenue[4] (covering 8.0 per cent of the aggregate Italian expenditures). The ratio to ordinary revenue remained substantially the same during the period considered. In the fiscal year 1934-35 these taxes represented 28 per cent of the ordinary revenue (covering 22 per cent of the total expenditures). To evaluate these figures, one must remember that direct taxes on individuals and corporations

---

[3] This scheme, which had some similarity to other proposals advanced in this country, was rather interesting, because it constituted a loan to the government (and was therefore anti-inflationary), and at the same time was a kind of insurance against monetary devaluation. The "privileged saver," according to official announcements, was to be granted the priority right to durable consumers goods or capital goods after the war, with the government guaranteeing the goods and prices. The Italian town population seemed to be attracted by the prospect of earmarking furniture, bicycles, cars, and radios, whereas agricultural instruments and building material appealed to the peasants. In either case, at the end of the war the privileged saver was to have a priority over other consumers.

The details of the project are not known, but the cause of its abandonment is easy to understand. The Italian people would certainly have liked to buy postwar goods at their 1942 prices, high as they were. Obviously, however, the government felt the impossibility of keeping such an engagement, in view of the inflationary process already well under way.

The idea of privileged saving was eventually used, or rather, distorted, by the government for quite a different purpose, i.e., to justify some of the compulsory investments to be enumerated later.

[4] In this paper, we consider as *ordinary revenue* only receipts from taxation, State monopolies, and lotteries.

in the United States yielded during the fiscal year 1942-43 69 per cent of federal gross receipts (in 1944 the ratio is expected to reach 78.8 per cent), covering 21 per cent of the total budget expenditures.

Italian receipts from direct taxes were 4.5 billion lire in 1934-35 and 10.8 billion in 1942-43.[5] The difference is partly due to increased revenue from existing taxes (because of monetary devaluation, economic expansion, etc.), partly to increased rates,[6] and partly to new taxes imposed to finance the war, and to fight inflation.

These new taxes may be divided into two categories: permanent and temporary. The first group includes a property tax and various levies on corporation dividends.

A permanent *property tax,* until then unknown to the Italian fiscal system, was passed in 1939, to become effective

---

5 According to the 1942-43 budget, they were estimated at 10.0 billion, 6.8 billion being derived from taxes existing in 1934, namely:

a. 5,250 million, *tax on incomes from "movable property,"* with rates ranging from 8 per cent on salaries, to 20 per cent on interest. The tax on salaries and wages was to be withheld by the employer.

b. 150 million, *land tax,* levied on the income received by the owner, after deduction of expenditures and losses. The rate was 10 per cent of the income (assessed in 1914 lire). Local government surtaxes may reach 950 per cent of the State tax, and actually amounted to about one billion.

c. 350 million, *tax on buildings,* levied on their net income. The rate was 10 per cent, but local government surtaxes may have amounted to 275 per cent of the State tax.

d. 810 million, *complementary tax on general income,* levied on incomes already subject to the three taxes mentioned above. Normal rates ranged from 1 to 10 per cent.

e. 240 million, *surtax on bachelors:* a tax with different rates varying according to the age, plus a surtax on the complementary tax on general income.

Some new taxes on capital gains were incorporated in existing taxes on transactions (see pages 173-74). Their revenue, however, was relatively unimportant.

6 Especially important is the case of the complementary tax on general income, whose rates were increased in June, 1940. The increases ranged from 25 per cent (for incomes of 10,000 lire) to 100 per cent (for incomes over 485,000 lire), the additional revenue being estimated at 240 million lire.

with the fiscal year 1940-41.[7] The yearly rate was established at 5 lire per thousand of the net estates. The burden on income, therefore, was 5, 10, and 16.6 per cent, when the property yielded an income of 10, 5, and 3 per cent respectively. The 1942-43 estimate amounted to 1.4 billion lire. The levy taxed the estates above 10,000 lire of all individuals, corporations, and unincorporated business, institutions, etc. Savings accounts and government securities were exempted.[8] The assessment was based on a three-year average of the current value of the estate.

Joint-stock company *dividends* have been subject to numerous restrictions and special taxes, which directly or indirectly reduced the purchasing power put into circulation through the distribution of corporation profits. Part of this purchasing power was directly absorbed through a 10 per cent tax on all dividends, interest coupons, bonuses and benefits (excluding those derived from government securities) accruing to bearer shareholders and bondholders (1936). This tax (withheld by the corporation at the time of the payment) was designed also to favor the conversion of bearer shares into registered shares, in order to limit the possibilities of tax evasion by individual investors. In December, 1940,

---

[7] See B. Cadalbert, "Sull'oggetto dell'imposta ordinaria sul patrimonio," in *Rivista Italiana di Diritto Finanziario,* 1940, p. 13 ff; E. Vanoni, "Chiose alle nuove imposte sul patrimonio e sulla entrata," in *Rivista di Diritto Finanziario e Scienza delle Finanze,* 1939, p. 22 ff. For a detailed and comparative survey in Italy and abroad, see *Associazione fra le Societa' per Azioni, L'imposta sul patrimonio in Italia ed all' Estero,* 1939.

[8] Practically all government securities in Italy are declared "exempt from any tax, present and future." This clause is interpreted so that interest on the public debt is exempt from the tax on incomes from "movable property," while it is subject to the complementary tax on general income. The exemption from the new property tax seems to be prompted essentially by political reasons, inasmuch as the exemption of savings accounts is justified for social reasons.

Another important group of properties exempted from normal taxation are the new buildings, exempted for 25 years from the tax on buildings. They are subject, however, to the new levy.

the rate was doubled to 20 per cent, and eventually imposed on all dividends, the registration of all shares having been made compulsory. In the 1942-43 budget revenue from this tax was estimated at 540 million lire.

Temporary direct taxes were imposed on war profits, on wages, and on compensations for corporation managers and directors. The most important among them was the *tax on excess war profits* derived from industrial or commercial activities, imposed in July, 1940; its yield in 1942-43 was estimated at 350 million. The 1938 income for individuals, and the average 1937-38 income for companies, were considered the normal income. If this was less than 8 per cent of the capital invested, the taxpayer could request that the "normal" income be raised to this limit. The rates varied from 10 per cent (for war profits exceeding the normal income by 20 per cent) to 60 per cent (for those exceeding the normal income by 100 per cent or more). Incomes below 12,000 lire were exempted.

In July, 1942, the tax-free portion of the total earnings was raised to 15,000 lire, and the amount of total earnings to which the excess war profits tax did not apply was raised from 6,000 to 8,000 lire. At the same time, the rate applying to the first groups was raised, so that the rates range now from 20 to 60 per cent. Moreover, the same decree ordered the compulsory investment in government securities of all remaining war profits, as mentioned above.[9]

In June, 1940, a flat 2 per cent *payroll tax* was imposed on small wages not subject to income tax, i.e., workers' incomes below 8,640 lire.[10] This tax, like the income tax on salaries

[9] See new consolidated text, published by R.D. 598, dated June 3, 1943.

[10] The statutory minimum income exempted from the tax on incomes from "movable property" was only 2,000 lire; actually, however, the administration exempted all wages below 720 lire monthly (and wage increases granted since 1939).

and wages, was to be withheld by the employer at the time of the payment. The yield, estimated at 240 million lire for the fiscal year 1942-43, was said to be designed to replenish the fund for the support of the families of men in the armed forces.

Since January, 1940, following the example set during the first World War, fees and other *remunerations of managers and directors of business concerns* were made subject to a special graduated surtax, with rates ranging from 10 per cent (for incomes between 10,000 and 20,000 lire) to 50 per cent (for incomes exceeding 50,000 lire). The tax (withheld by the corporation at the time of the payment) was estimated to yield in 1942-43 only 60 million lire.

Transfer and Sales Taxes

Indirect taxes on business transactions, which yielded in 1934-35 3.6 billion lire, representing 22 per cent of the ordinary revenue (and 17 per cent of the total Italian expenditures) in 1942-43 produced 11.3 billion, representing 30 per cent of the ordinary revenues (and 8.4 per cent of the total expenditures).

Most of the increase was due to the 1940 reorganization of the existing sales tax into a general 2 per cent *turnover tax,*[11] whose yield in the 1942-43 budget was estimated at 5.6 billion, compared with the 1.1 billion yield of the 1934-35 sales tax. The new tax absorbed in 1941-42 about 4 per cent of the national income, the highest proportion among large countries imposing such levies.

While the old sales tax was imposed (with various rates from .5 to 12 per cent) only on transactions between producers,

---

11 See E. Vanoni, "Chiose alle nuove imposte sul patrimonio e sulla entrata," in *Rivista di Diritto Finanziario e Scienza delle Finanze,* p. 32 ff.

between producers and merchants, and between merchants, the new levy was a tax on all monetary items in gross receipts for sales, services and the like. The tax was imposed not only on transactions previously subject to the sales tax, but also on sales to the final consumer, as well as on gross receipts of farmers, landowners, professional men, et al. The only exemptions were bread, daily newspapers, salaries and wages, interests and dividends paid by the State and local governments, and incomes from the sale of exported goods. The tax was paid every time the goods changed hands, so that the real burden averaged about 5 per cent of the retail price.[12] It was generally paid through special stamps, to be applied to invoices, receipts, and the like; above a certain amount, by means of deposit in special Treasury accounts; sometimes, especially for professional services, the tax was met by a fixed annual payment individually agreed upon by the administration. In some fields of production or of trade, collective agreements established the payment in relation to the income assessed for the tax on incomes from "movable property," thus transforming the new levy into a surtax on that particular tax.

In June, 1943, with a view to curbing inflation, increasing the ordinary budget revenue, and ensuring the service of the public debt, a wartime surtax was added to the existing turnover tax. It was expected to yield at least 3 additional billion per year. On all transactions, except retail sales, the new surtax was levied at the rate of 1 per cent of the gross receipts. On retail transactions the rate was 1.2 per cent, calculated not on the retail selling price, but on the retailer's buying price. In the case of professional and other services on which the basic turnover tax was met by an annual payment, this pay-

12 E. Vanoni (*ibid.*, p. 38-39) examines a typical case of cotton fabric, where the burden can reach 6.85 per cent of the retail price.

ment was increased by 50 per cent to cover the new surtax. The decree imposing the surtax provided for certain exemptions, including imports not subject to the basic turnover tax. It was stated that this surtax had to be paid by the receiver of the income and could not be passed on to the purchaser, consumer, tenant, etc., who was to continue to be liable only for the basic turnover tax of 2 per cent.

The group of taxes on transactions includes also some progressive taxes on capital gains, which in Italy are not always subject to ordinary income taxes. Through these taxes the Fascist government tried to discourage two consequences of inflation (investment and speculation in real estate and in stocks), while at the same time favoring investments in government securities.[13]

In addition to the normal 6 per cent registration tax, in June, 1940, a new special tax was imposed in order to curb the realization of *real estate capital gains.* The rate was set at 60 per cent of the increment in value, granting, however, an exemption basis of 300,000 lire. In September, 1941, while the normal registration tax was increased from 6 to 8 per cent, the exemption basis for the assessment of the special 60 per cent tax was reduced from 300,000 to 50,000 lire. The yearly revenue (which in 1940 had been estimated at some 15 million) was expected to be somewhat increased. The reason for the change was essentially a technical one, the government aiming primarily not at siphoning purchasing power, but at discouraging speculation by absorbing a very large portion of the profit. The system, however, was further changed in April, 1943, when the special tax was abolished by a new Minister of Finance, and merged into the normal regis-

[13] The Fascist government obstructed completely the third way classically chosen by people trying to avoid the frightful consequences of monetary devaluation: it forbade any trade in precious stones and metals, except for industrial purposes.

tration tax, with increased and progressive rates, ranging from 3 to 30 per cent.[14]

3 per cent on values up to 5,000 lire;
12 per cent on values over 5,000 but not exceeding 100,000 lire;
20 per cent on values over 100,000 but not exceeding 500,000 lire;
25 per cent on values over 500,000 but not exceeding 5 million lire;
30 per cent on values over 5 million lire.

To curb excess investments on the Italian stock exchanges, which had caused an exceptional boom, a decree was passed in July, 1941, which ordered *capital gains from stock deals* to be subject to a graduated tax, similar to analogous duties imposed in other countries.[15] The new tax, which did not affect the existing levies on share turnovers, was charged to the seller, and applied to all transactions carried on or outside the stock exchange, on a cash or forward basis, in shares. The rates were established as follows: 10 per cent on profits up to 10 per cent; 30 per cent on profits from 10 to 40 per cent; and 50 per cent on profits exceeding 40 per cent.[16] All profits deriving from deals in shares of real estate companies were subject to a flat 60 per cent rate, corresponding to the rate established for the newly imposed tax on real estate plus-values (see above).

The new stock profits tax, however, did not check the investment trends nor the upward movement on the stock ex-

---

14 They were established by progressive degrees on a sliding scale as follows:

15 For French, German, and Japanese examples, see *Bank of International Settlements, 1941-1942 Report,* p. 194, and A. Amato, "La Nuova imposta sul plus-valore dei titoli azionari nella finanza di guerra Italiana," in *Rivista di Diritto Finanziario e Scienza delle Finanze,* 1941, p. 167.

16 In the case of shares which had been purchased before October 31, 1940, taxable profit was considered to be the difference between the sale price and the price prevailing at that date, thus exempting from the new levy all increases in value occurred before Italy's entering into the World conflict, or in the first months after it.

changes.[17] Consequently the graduate rates were abolished after a little more than two months (September 27, 1941), and replaced by a flat 20 per cent tax on profits, to be paid by the seller, plus a 4 per cent turnover surtax on the share value, to be paid by the purchaser. An immediate decline in quotations accompanied the new decree, followed, however, by a recovery. In spite of the fact that the tax was legally imposed on the seller, it is believed that its economic burden was shifted to the purchaser, because of the decreasing amounts of shares offered on the market.[18] Eventual fluctuations of the market were not determined by fiscal reasons. On April, 1943, the new Minister of Finance abolished this tax on stock profits, while he increased the 4 per cent turnover surtax to a normal 3 per cent of the nominal value, plus 20 per cent of the price in excess of it. It was established, however, that the rate might be raised to 60 per cent by Ministerial decree, according to the position of the market, and in the first application of the new decree the rate was in fact fixed at 35 per cent. This was followed by a notable increase in turnover and prices. The same decree abolished the obligation mentioned below for every purchaser of shares, to invest in an equivalent amount of special 3 per cent Treasury bonds.

---

17 Apparently, this was the result of a shrinkage of supply, coupled with steady demand in all sections of the market. Moreover, because the new tax applied only to the seller, the investing public preferred holding its shares, a technical position favorable to further price rises being thus created. (See Borgatta Gino, in Borgatta and others, *Ricostruzione dell' Economia nel Dopoguerra,* 1942, p. 79, footnote.) The share prices index had risen in the second half of July, 1941, from 329.37 to 360.50, which was 140 points higher than in June, 1940. The decrease in supply was reflected in a decline in turnover, the daily average amounting to 129,020 shares against 161,489 shares in the first half of July. See *Neue Zuercher Zeitung,* August 3, 1941.

18 See A. Amato, *ibid.,* pp. 168-69. The same applies also to the tax on real estate plus-values.

Taxes on Consumption

In the group of *customs and excise duties* the impact of the war was not very significant, except for a decrease in the revenue from customs duties (from 3.1 billion lire in 1934-35, to 2.3 billion, estimated in the 1942-43 budget) as a consequence of the shrinking foreign trade, largely compensated for by the increase in the revenue from excise duties (from 1.8 to 3.8 billion during the same period) chiefly due to increased prices, and to a heavier levy imposed on the refining of mineral oils (from 174 to 1,100 million).

The importance of this group of taxes in relation to the total ordinary revenue, however, decreased from 30 per cent in the fiscal year 1934-35 (when they covered 23 per cent of the total expenditures), to 16 per cent in 1942-43 (covering 4.5 per cent of the total expenditures). During the same period the net fiscal revenue of *government monopolies* (tobacco, salt, matches and lighting appliances, and cigarette paper) increased from 2.9 to 8.2 billion, representing 18 and 22 per cent, respectively, of the ordinary revenue (and covering 14 and 6.1 per cent, respectively, of the total expenditures). The gross revenue from *lotteries* increased from 450 million lire (2.7 per cent of the ordinary revenue) to 673 million (1.8 per cent of the ordinary revenue).

On the whole, indirect taxes on consumption increased during the period considered from 8.3 to 15.0 billion lire. Their relative importance decreased from 50 per cent of the ordinary revenue in 1934-35 (when they covered 40 per cent of the national expenditures) to 40 per cent in 1942-43 (when they covered 11 per cent of the national expenditures).

If we consider indirect taxation as a whole (taxes on business transactions and taxes on consumption together) we find that the revenue therefrom increased during the period considered from 11.9 to 26.3 billion lire, approximately the same ratio of expansion which marked the whole of ordinary revenue. In 1934-35 these taxes represented 73 per cent of the ordinary revenue (covering 57 per cent of the total national expenditures) and in 1942-43 they represented 71 per cent of the ordinary revenue (covering 19 per cent of the national expenditures).

The disproportionate burden of indirect taxation on low income groups is well known. The somewhat analogous category of "miscellaneous internal revenue" in this country represented in 1942-43 19 per cent of the total federal receipts, covering 6 per cent of the aggregate budget expenditures.

Capital Levies

In addition to the taxes mentioned above, three capital levies were imposed in 1936, 1937, and 1938, to pay for the expenses of the Ethiopian adventure.[19] The first was a 5 per cent forced loan levied on *real-estate owners*.[20] All owners of

19 The Italian money had been devaluated in 1936 by 41 per cent. The Fascist Minister of Finance Thaon di Revel explained (May 18, 1938) that the capital levies fell on those who had "gained" by the devaluation. It is evident, however, that the "gain" of real estate owners, shareholders and the like, as a direct consequence of the devaluation, consisted only in a larger monetary expression of the unchanged economic value of their property. It was, therefore, an illusory gain, which could appear real only in the light of the decreased purchasing power of the fixed incomes. The real justification of these capital levies, therefore, was the need of funds to finance war expenditures and the necessity of siphoning off inflationary purchasing power for war purposes.

The only precedent for forced loans to be found in Italy's financial history occurred in 1866, to pay the expenses of the war for independence against Austria. In that year a 400 million lire (face value) loan was subscribed to under compulsion by people paying direct taxes (tax on land, tax on building, and tax on incomes from "movable property"), with progressive quotas being applied to their ordinary assessments. The redemption of that loan by the Treasury was completed in 1880.

20 For a detailed discussion of this levy see F. Flora, "Il prestito e la proprieta' fondiaria," in *Rivista di Diritto Finanziario e Scienza delle Finanze,* 1937, p. 8 ff; J. Griziotti Kretschmann, "Caratteri finanziari distintivi del prestito—imposta immobiliare," *ibid.,* p. 25 ff; V. Bompani, *Il nuovo prestito redimibile 5% e l'imposta straordinaria sulla proprieta' immobiliare,* 1937; G. Capodaglio,

real estate—except the national government, local governments, and benevolent and some other institutions named in the Decree of October 5, 1936, were obliged to subscribe to this loan a sum equal to at least 5 per cent of the value of their real property.[21] The funds necessary for the service of this loan, moreover, were secured by the enactment, as from January 1, 1937, for a period of twenty-five years, of an extraordinary tax at the rate of .35 per cent on the value of the real estate as assessed for the loan.[22] The first levy, therefore, had only the form of a loan. Its burden through this extraordinary tax was made to fall exclusively on these same land and building owners.

In order to facilitate the subscription to this capital levy, banks were authorized to make advances up to 90 per cent of the levy, and a special form of insurance was established by the State-controlled National Insurance Institute to cover the fiscal duty of subscribing to the loan. Only big owners, however, had recourse to these facilities. According to Thaon di Revel's statement of May 18, 1938, the yield of this capital levy, as of March 31, 1938, was 7 billion lire, as against a

---

"Caratteristiche del prestito obbligatorio sulla proprieta' immobiliare," in *Rivista Italiana di Scienze Economiche,* November, 1936; R. Ossola, "Osservazioni sul nuovo Contributo Straordinario Immobiliare," in *Giornale degli Economisti,* February, 1937; A. Deni, "Prestito Redimibile ed imposta straordinaria immobiliare," in *Rivista Italiana di Diritto Finanziario,* 1937, p. 363 ff.

21 The value of the real estate was to be estimated as follows: (1) The cadastral value of plots of land subject, or to become subject, to the land tax, was multiplied by a fixed coefficient of 3.66, and capitalized at 5 per cent; (2) The rent of buildings, subject, or to become subject, to the corresponding tax, was capitalized at 5 per cent. The 3.66 coefficient, applied to the value of plots of land, corresponds to the monetary devaluation which followed the first World War, the cadastral value being assessed in 1914 lire. Estates under 10,000 lire were exempted. This exemption covered 36 per cent of the value of Italian lands, and 25 per cent of the value of buildings subject to normal taxes.

22 In the 1942-43 budget, the yield of this extraordinary tax on real estate was estimated at 500 million lire.

total of 7.5 billion entered on the rolls.[23] Of this sum, 4.4 billion had been paid out of current income, or savings of subscribers; 1.1 billion out of advances made by banks or by insurance companies out of available reserves; and 1.4 billion by means of banknotes issued by the Bank of Italy in response to applications received. It is believed, however, that this inflationary circuit was eventually closed with satisfactory rapidity through the repayments made by subscribers who had recourse to credit. Obviously, this reabsorption of excess purchasing power was facilitated—in this, as in the case of the other capital levies mentioned below—by the increase in prices and money incomes due to the 1936 devaluation of the lire, and by the expansion of economic activity due to the increase in public expenditures for armaments.[24] The taxpayer was entitled to proceed to the redemption of the extraordinary .35 per cent tax, with a 10 per cent discount.[25]

A second capital levy was imposed on corporations in October, 1937.[26] This was a 10 per cent tax on the *capital and reserves of joint stock companies,* as of October 5, 1936, with the following exemptions: (1) shares of other companies, in order to avoid double taxation; (2) immovable

23 On April 17, 1941, however, at a hearing before the Budget Committee of the Chamber of Deputies the same Minister gave the figure of 6,405 million as the yield of this compulsory loan and its contribution to meeting the deficit from 1935 to 1941.

24 See Gino Borgatta, in Borgatta and others, *Ricostruzione dell 'Economia nel Dopoguerra,* 1942, p. 97, footnote.

25 For the school favoring redemption of all "consolidated" taxes, in order to curb inflation, see B. Griziotti, "Riscatto delle imposte ammortizzabili e nuove finanze di guerra," in *Rivista di Diritto Finanziario e Scienza delle Finanze,* 1941, p. 17 ff., and bibliography therein; *do. do.* "Politica e finanza di guerra," *ibid.,* p. 87 ff. For the theoretical angles of the problem, see C. Shoup, "Capitalization and Shifting of the Property Tax," in *Property Taxes,* Tax Policy League, 1940, p. 187.

26 See details in B. Griziotti, "Profilo scientifico e giuridico dell 'imposta straordinaria sul capitale delle società per azioni," in *Rivista di Diritto Finanziario e Scienza delle Finanze,* 1937, p. 353 ff.

properties, already subject to the real estate levy; (3) government securities. Furthermore, banks were completely exempted. The levy was to be paid in 15 installments during 1938, 1939, and 1940. The government favored the immediate payment of the levy, with an 8 per cent discount; banks were authorized to make advances up to 80 per cent of the amount due. By this process, similar to that provided for the real estate levy, the specially created inflationary purchasing power was to be reabsorbed by the year 1940.

Two alternatives were also offered to companies having no liquid funds: (1) They were authorized to pay 50 per cent of the capital levy by a corresponding increase of their capital, and by handing over the new shares to the Treasury; or (2) They were authorized to ask their shareholders for the necessary cash and then to make a corresponding increase of their capital. To facilitate this operation, they were authorized to revalue their assets on the basis of the new value of the lira, and to distribute this apparent surplus value to the shareholders, in the form of free shares, equal in amount to double that raised by the issuance of shares against cash. The majority of large companies took advantage of the second possibility, which was psychologically attractive, and fiscally profitable.[27]

The levy, however, was bound to reduce in any case the

---

[27] Actually, the shareholders scarcely realized that they were going to have a loss, through the levy on the capital of their corporation. They even felt as if they were receiving a benefit, because they received two shares free, for each share subscribed and paid for in cash. In fact, they could sell their rights, and have in this way an immediate gain, without realizing the reduction in their equity position because of the levy.

The operation offered also two tax advantages: (a) the possibility of distributing higher dividends, without paying the progressive penalty rate established for dividends over 6 per cent; and (b) the increase in the yearly amortization sums allowed to be deducted from gross income in the determination of the net taxable income of the company.

The stock exchange was dull before the announcement of the levy because heavier levies were expected but revived briskly for a few months after the decree was published.

shareholder's income, because the decree ordered that 20 per cent of the annual income of the corporation was thereafter to be accumulated until this special reserve would equal the levy paid, either in cash or in shares. The total yield of this levy, originally estimated at 5 to 6 billion lire, in the preparation of the 1938-39 budget was revised downward to 3 billion only (of which, 1.8 billion was to be collected in that fiscal year).[28]

The series of capital levies was completed by a decree, dated November 9, 1938, which established an extraordinary 7.5 per cent levy on the *capital of industrial and commercial business,* owned by individuals or by non-incorporated partnerships, including cooperatives.[29] Concerns having an income below 10,000 lire were exempted. The basis of the levy was the 1938 income (as assessed for the tax on incomes from movable property, cat. B) capitalized at 8 per cent. This was to be reduced, however, by sliding rates ranging from 55 to 30 per cent, for industrial enterprises, and from 70 to 45 per cent, for commercial enterprises, in order to limit the capitalization of income to that part considered to be derived from capital and to exclude that part derived from management or the owner's labor. The levy was to be paid in three to five years, depending upon its relative burden, compared with the normal income tax.[30] A discount of 8 per cent per year was granted to taxpayers for the payment in advance of the whole levy.

---

28 In explaining this reduction to the Senate, the Minister stated that it showed the "moderation" with which the tax had been applied, in order not to place too heavy a burden on the Italian industry.

29 See S. Steve, "L'Imposta Straordinaria sul Capitale delle aziende industriali e commerciali," in *Rivista di Diritto Finanziario e Scienza delle Finanze,* 1938, p. 399 ff.

30 The yearly quota of the levy could not exceed five-fourths of the 1938 income tax.

Compulsory Loans

Forced saving, in the British manner, was not resorted to by the Fascists, because of the acknowledged extremely low level of Italian wages. However, compulsory investment in government securities and forced loans were ordered on several occasions.

In many cases, the investment in government securities was made compulsory for political or social reasons. Several instances are to be found in the field of social security and of life insurance and employees' indemnity funds, where the statutes provided for the automatic investment of reserves in government securities. But since there was no issue of special bonds, these instances are not generally considered as "forced loans."

Another example of compulsory investment prompted primarily by non-inflationary reasons may be found in the confiscation of foreign securities held by Italian citizens. They were ordered to exchange these securities for nine-year 5 per cent Italian Treasury bonds in December, 1935, when the Fascist government was badly in need of foreign exchange. Still another instance was the seizure of Jewish property against special nontransferable 4 per cent Treasury bonds. This was ordered in 1938, when anti-Jewish laws were passed. It was anticipated that the seizure would bring in perhaps 2 billion lire.

In several other cases, the order for compulsory investment in government securities was primarily inspired by the desire to combat the inflationary pressure of excess purchasing power. In October, 1942, for instance, the Fascist government doubled the *family allowances* of the men under arms. In order to avoid inflationary effect, however, the government provided that these sums were to be invested in nontransferable Treasury bonds, as a form of obligatory savings.[31]

Similarly the Fascist government tried to counteract the inflationary pressure of *excess war profits* through compulsory investment in government securities. According to a decree dated June 23, 1942, all excess profits due to the war (i.e., the difference between current and "normal" profits, less the amount already paid in extra and normal taxation and a small amount representing a fraction of the ordinary profit) were to be invested in a special type of registered Treasury bonds, which were not to be transferable before the end of the war.[32] The law applied to all earnings exceeding 50,000 lire, and was retroactive to 1939. It was announced that the use of the sums so invested would be decided upon at the end of the war and that preference would be given to expenditures for plants, for reconversion or reconstruction purposes, and to reconstitution of stocks.

In order to discourage stock exchange investments, as well as inflationary transfers of purchasing power from *joint-stock companies* to individuals, another 1942 decree ordered that upon the establishment of new companies, or upon increases in the capital of existing companies, at least 20 per cent of the subscribed or new capital was to be invested in a special series of 3 per cent registered nine-year Treasury bonds. These bonds were not transferable until the death of the holder, or the liquidation or merging of the company. If the capital increase took place by a rise in the nom-

---

31 It was difficult, at a time when the cost of living was sharply rising, to reconcile this compulsory investment with the justification of subsidies to needy families. Yet, Italian officials followed here the line of reasoning for "privileged" saving, asserting that the accumulation had been ordered for the benefit of the families concerned "in order to facilitate the return to normal conditions at the end of the war."

32 In the case of corporations and other companies, however, after payment of a small fee, these Treasury certificates might be transferred from the company to the partners or shareholders, within certain limits.

inal value of the shares, an amount equal to 50 per cent of the nominal newly created value was to be subscribed in new Treasury bonds within a month by the shareholder. If the capital increase was effected by the issuance of new shares below the market value, an amount equal to 20 per cent of the capital increase, plus 50 per cent of the total value of the shareholder's subscription rights was to be invested in the new Treasury bonds. If the capital increase occurred through the issue of new shares at market value, 20 per cent of the increase was to be subscribed.

An effort was made to curb at the same time one of the causes (excess purchasing power) and one of the effects (stock exchange boom) of the inflationary situation through a special decree, December, 1942. This ordered any purchaser of industrial or commercial shares listed on the Italian *stock exchange* to subscribe to an equal amount of 3 per cent blocked Treasury bonds.[33] This edict, however, proved to be too drastic. It resulted in complete market stagnation, which ceased only when the decree was repealed after a few months (May, 1943), by the new Minister of Finance. He established a new tax payable by the seller, which has already been described.

Conclusions

The preceding summary description of the main fiscal instruments used by the Fascist government shows that Italy's policies during this period were certainly not hindered by lack of technical machinery. As already mentioned in the introduction, the inflationary process actually started in 1940, when Mussolini decided to participate in World War II, and was to a considerable extent under control up

[33] Shares not listed officially on the stock exchange were to be subject only to a 4 per cent turnover tax, payable in equal parts by the buyer and the seller.

to the end of 1942. When the Allied military pressure began to be increasingly felt through air bombing, the Italian situation developed into economic and political disruption and finally resulted in total disintegration.

It is difficult to evaluate the Fascist attempts to limit monetary circulation and to curb price inflation—fair as their results may appear in comparison with the galloping inflationary process which is now under way, as a consequence of the latest political and military developments. No doubt some of the fiscal devices adopted by the Fascist ministers between 1935 and 1943 are interesting from a technical viewpoint. Their application, however, was not efficient; in fact it was timid, partly because the government felt the lack of cooperation of the Italian people, whose heart was not in the war against the Allies, either in the battlefronts or in the economic and financial fields.

At the end of the period considered, in the fiscal year 1942-43, the ordinary revenue covered only 27 per cent of the total state expenditures. Between 1935 and 1943 the aggregate ordinary and miscellaneous revenue was increased only to match the expanded ordinary expenditures, including a part of the increase of the burden for interest charges.[34] War expenditures were met by borrowing (a substantial part of it, perhaps 50 billion lire, through potentially inflationary short-term Treasury notes)[35] and by the inflationary

34 Ordinary revenue in 1934-35 was 16.4 billion lire, and in 1942-43 was 37.2 billion; effective ordinary expenditures (excluding war expenses) amounted in the same fiscal years to 20.8 and 54.1 billion lire. However, taking into account miscellaneous revenue, the ordinary deficit increased only from 2.0 to 5.2 billion, exclusive of war expenditures. These ordinary deficits include all interest charges (which are an item of the ordinary budget); during the period considered, payments for interest on public debt increased, due to the war borrowing, by 8.3 billion lire.

35 The Italian domestic public debt, as it appears from official statistics, increased by 316 per cent (102.6 billion lire in June, 1934, and 426 billion in June, 1943). But while in 1934 the consolidated or long-term debt constituted

creation of fiat money by the Bank of Italy. In the last part of the period considered, issue of fiat money developed on such an unprecedented scale as to overpower existing controls. The monetary circulation,[36] which from 13.1 billion lire at the end of 1934 had increased to 24.4 billion at the close of 1939,[37] amounted to 86.2 billion at the end of June, 1943, and to 96.6 billion on July 31, 1943.[38]

As for price inflation, data are not available about the exact rise of the Italian price level and cost of living, because no indexes have been published by Italian authorities in the last years. All evidence, however, points to the fact that they followed a similar trend. According to an authoritative estimate,[39] the cost of living increased by 65 per cent between 1934 and 1940, if one excludes the black market. It was only after 1940, however, that the inflationary factors assumed increasing importance. After Italy's active participation in World War II, observers noticed a violent acceleration in the upward movement of prices paid in the normal market, and at the same time an overgrowth of the black market, where the increase in prices was even more accentuated.

A cost-of-living index reflecting the prices actually paid at the end of the period considered (July, 1943), therefore, would certainly show that wage earners and consumers suf-

---

90 per cent of the entire public debt, in 1943 it was only 20 or 25 per cent of it. Of the remaining 75 or 80 per cent, the short-term ordinary Treasury bonds (one- to twelve-months notes) mentioned in the text are particularly significant from the inflationary standpoint.

36 In aiming at a better understanding of the significance of these figures, one should not ignore the State note circulation (small denominations) which may be estimated at from 10 to 20 billion lire.

37 The circulation at the end of 1937 was 17.5 billion, the increase being mostly justified by the 1936 devaluation, when the gold content of the lira was decreased by 41 per cent.

38 Since September, 1943, Italy has had two separate inflationary processes, one in the North and the other in the South. In German-occupied Italy not less than 50 billion paper lire were reported issued between September and November, 1943.

39 *The Economist,* December 27, 1941, p. 786-87.

fered in Italy more than in any other major country. Evidently, the "circuit of capital"[40] was not welded. Neither the siphoning off of surplus purchasing power through taxes and borrowing, nor the very strict rationing of all essential commodities, nor subsidies, nor totalitarian blocking of commodity prices, wages, and rents, could prevent the inflationary distortion of the whole economic system, when external military pressure gave increased speed and weight to the spiralling factors in the Italian economy.

---

[40] The theory of the circuit of capital was persistently expounded by Thaon di Revel, Minister of Finance during most of the period examined. With that term, borrowed from the vocabulary of electricity, and with the aid of some well known economic concepts like Keynes' multiplier and the principle of acceleration, Fascist theorists proclaimed that the money spent by the state for economically reproductive purposes goes back to the Treasury, or is absorbed in widened business activity, without any inflationary effect. They assumed, moreover, that inflation could be avoided, even in the case of war expenses, if the capital sums made available were invested in public bonds. If such investment does not take place, the circuit is not welded, and to transfer purchasing power from the individual to the state it then becomes necessary either to impose new taxes or to issue new fiat money. Fascist economists emphasized, therefore, the importance of the psychological factor, which is supposed, if favorable, to prevent capital from flying out of the circuit. At the same time, however, they went on to point out that it is almost impossible to achieve a perfect welding of the circuit when expenditures are very large, because of the ever-increasing time interval between the moment of expenditure by the state and the moment purchasing power is eventually reabsorbed.

CHAPTER XV

CANADIAN EXPERIENCE IN CURBING INFLATION THROUGH FISCAL DEVICES

A. Kenneth Eaton

Chief of Tax Investigation, Department of Finance, Canada

In wartime the government itself through its spending program creates the inflation problem. It is, then, clearly up to the government to deal directly with it. Our government in Canada recognized this duty at the outset. In the first war budget of September, 1939, control of inflation formed an integral part of the financial program outlined at that time. A pattern of fiscal policy was then set which for five years has been closely adhered to. The treatment, most Canadian taxpayers will agree, has been drastic but, at the same time, it is probable that they would likewise agree that the policy has been justified by results.

Prewar Control of Deflation

It may be of interest in passing to mention that our experience with taxation as an instrument of economic control has not been limited to the war period in Canada. Just prior to the outbreak of war we were engaged in an experiment with taxation as a means of combatting not inflation but deflation. As you will recall, the tense international situation in the spring of 1939 was playing havoc with plans for business expansion.

In the face of this threatened decline we offered at that

time, under the corporation income tax, a substantial credit against taxes as a reward for capital expenditure in the following twelve-month period. For every $100 of immediate capital outlay a company would be entitled to receive a $10 credit against its tax bill, the credit to be spread forward evenly over the next three years. Shortly stated, Treasury money in a critical period was used to assist on a 10 per cent basis in financing private capital expenditure to combat deflationary forces.

How successful devices of this kind are it is always difficult to say. Results are hard to measure, but in this instance we believe that the tax incentive was an important factor in inducing the construction activity which followed. Control devices of this sort, however, are expensive. You have to pay not only for the *increase* in capital outlay but also for the capital outlay which in the absence of any tax incentive would in any case have been undertaken. It is difficult to give tax credit only where credit is due.

Wartime Fiscal Policy Outlined

From a prewar monetary and fiscal policy designed to combat deflation we were shortly forced to reverse our front and train our guns on an enemy approaching in the opposite direction. In the first war budget in September, 1939, a fiscal program for the war was outlined in which it was anticipated that there would be different stages of development, each with its appropriate fiscal policy. The first phase was that of speeding up the wheels of industry, and reaching as soon as possible a condition of full employment of our resources. The situation in this initial period justified only moderate increases in revenue taxes, although the occasion was used to broaden the tax base to serve as an indication that everybody was going to have to help to pay for the war.

The speeding up of economic activity with the emergency of real as distinct from artificial or temporary scarcities indicated that the second main stage had been reached. At this point the government opened its main drive for heavy tax revenue. The objectives were twofold: (1) to pay as we go as far as possible; and (2) to get as many dollars as possible out of the hands of the spenders. I shall not inflict upon you the details of successive war budgets. The facts which are significant will appear most clearly, I think, through a brief statement of present tax levels with some prewar comparisons.

Comparison of Present and Prewar Tax Levels

Before the war a single man receiving $1,800 a year paid $24 Dominion income tax. He now pays just under $500 if he is not currently paying insurance, into a pension fund or on the principal of a mortgage on his home. Savings in these three directions are allowed as offsets against the refundable portion of the tax. Against the $500 tax just mentioned the maximum offset or refundable portion is $144. In the case of a married person without dependents earning $1,800 there was in the prewar period no tax, whereas the present law compels a payment of $343, half of which may be offset or refunded.

At the $3,000 level the single man used to pay $70. Under present rates he must give up $1,064, or more than one-third of his salary. This tax of over $1,000 may be offset to the extent of only $240. The married man with no dependents receiving $3,000 used to pay only $30 tax, 1 per cent of his income. Our new rates take $884 from him which is more than 29 per cent of his salary. In this the refundable portion is $300.

Moving up the scale to the $5,000 level the prewar tax on a single man, incredible as it sounds today, was $180 only.

Present rates take $2,128 or over 42½ per cent of his earnings, and only $400 of this may be offset or returned to him. The married man with no dependents now pays a tax of $1,878 on an income of $5,000. He may offset $500 of this.

Present rates may take $5,112 out of $10,000 earned by a single man, leaving him less than half of his income. The offset at this level is limited to $800. A married man with $10,000 must still pay $3,760 after he has used his offsets.

The government leaves the $50,000 man about $15,000, and the $100,000 man about $20,000 out of which to buy bonds.

Generally speaking, our individual income taxes are at about the same level as those in Great Britain. Where the taxpayer has no voluntary savings as offsets ours in many cases are more severe. Some useful comparisons of tax levels in the United Kingdom, the United States, and Canada have been published by your Treasury Department, and the *Federal Reserve Bulletin* has recently made a similar study.

The corporate tax picture in Canada is easily summed up. Before the war the tax rate was 15 per cent. Now corporation income tax and excess profits tax combined take 40 per cent as a minimum and where profits are more than about 17 per cent above prewar standard the government takes everything above this point, and will unconditionally return 20 per cent of it after the war. No company in Canada today can retain more than 70 per cent of its prewar standard profits.

So much for the main direct taxes. I shall now mention some of the chief indirect taxes on commodities and services.

The tax on spirits which was $4 per gallon before the war is now $11 per gallon. The tax on malt used in making beer has been moved up from 6c to 16c per pound. The tax on cigarettes has gone up from $4 to $10 per thousand, which means that in buying a package of twenty cigarettes you contribute more than 20c to the government. Many cigarette smokers have reverted to the somewhat inconvenient process of rolling their own, but even here they do not escape the government's hand. Taxes have added 20 per cent to the cost of amusements and 15 per cent to the cost of travel. A 25 per cent tax is levied on practically all electrical household appliances, refrigerators, cameras, phonographs and cosmetics, where any are left to sell. Candy and chewing gum carry a tax of 30 per cent. Soft drinks are 2c per bottle higher in price because of taxes. Trunks, suitcases, smokers' accessories and fountain pens, bear a 35 per cent tax. A tax of 1½c is added to the price of sugar, and 3c a gallon applies to gasoline in addition to provincial taxes, which run as high as 10c a gallon, making 13c combined. The above mentioned taxes are generally at the manufacturers' level and usually are in addition to the 8 per cent sales tax.

In the 1942 budget we experimented at the retail level with taxes of 25 per cent on jewelry, clocks, watches, cut glass and china. Imports from hard currency countries bear a 10 per cent war exchange tax. Postage has been increased by 1c. The above enumerated taxes by no means exhaust the list, but they are indicative of the type of taxes used, and of the general level of the rates. Many of them will sound familiar to you.

Sales Tax Not Increased

In view of certain discussion in this country you may be interested in the fact that since the war we have not increased the rate of our general sales tax. It still stands at the prewar level of 8 per cent. It is a very productive tax and, levied at the manufacturers' level, it is relatively inexpensive to collect. You might naturally ask why, with this efficient tax collecting machinery already at hand operating smoothly, more use has not been made of it, particularly as a means of inflation control. This deserves some comment.

In our first three war budgets there were no technical or practical obstacles in the way of extending our use of the sales tax, but as a matter of policy it was left practically untouched. Right from the initial formulation of a war finance program the government has asserted, and reasserted, that every attempt would be made to spread the burden of war taxation fairly and according to ability to bear it. The government believed the income tax to be a more equitable method of raising revenue than the general sales tax and in the light of its declared policy left the latter untouched.

Price and Wage Ceilings

Between the third and fourth war budgets it had become very obvious that something more than a drastic taxing policy was needed to prevent a general price rise, and in the autumn of 1941 a ceiling on prices and wages and salaries was imposed, with concurrent provision for compulsory cost-of-living bonuses for wage earners. With a frozen price structure, only a moment's consideration reveals the difficulties in the way of any subsequent increase in a general sales tax which is imposed at the manufacturers' level. Assuming that an adjustment of prices would be allowed, to follow through the appropriate price increases due to tax alone from the manufacturer right down to the consumer would have been next to impossible. Furthermore, the higher resulting price to the consumer would have provided the basis for a corresponding increase in the cost-of-living bonus, and this in turn would bring a labor cost "squeeze" on the employer who is operating under a fixed selling price for his goods. With this picture before us, I repeat, we did not increase the sales tax in our latest budgets. Whether but for this price ceiling obstacle it would have been increased in the last two budgets I cannot say, and governments rarely answer hypothetical questions.

What I have said up to now has been mainly intended to establish the one fact that the government in Canada has been doing a quite thorough job of taking spending money out of the pockets of the people. Tax policy has, I think, been given a fair try as a means of combating inflation. At this point I should like to make some general observations from our experience and assess the importance of the tax instruments in combating inflation, pointing out at the same time certain definite limitations imposed on its use.

Role of Taxation in Combating Inflation

Price increases may be said to come about broadly in two ways. On the one hand prices may be pulled up by consumer demand and by sellers adopting a policy of charging what the traffic will bear. Perhaps this is the most commonly accepted idea of the inflationary process; that is, we ordinarily think of an enormously expanded amount of consumer income paid out by the government being spent on a limited supply of goods, with inflation coming about through the excess demand. On the other hand, prices may be pushed up through higher labor costs. We have the two forces at work, one a pull, the other a push. In the attack against inflation, then, we must fight on two fronts. Taxation may be used to cut down consumer demand, but a price and wage ceiling is needed to prevent costs from pushing up prices.

Of these methods of combating inflation it is obvious, I think, that the price and wage ceiling, and particularly the latter, is by far the more fundamental. The most that taxation can do is to relieve the pressure on price ceilings by reducing purchasing power. But while taxation may relieve pressure on price ceilings it very definitely increases the pressure against wage and salary ceilings. This latter point, which is frequently overlooked, cannot be too strongly emphasized. In the absence of a frozen price and wage structure it is possible under certain conditions that heavy taxation on balance may accelerate rather than retard the inflationary process. Perhaps it would be worth while to elaborate this point.

In 1940 the Canadian government imposed a very moderate tax, called a national defense tax, which went right down to the first dollar of income in the case of incomes over certain levels and was deducted from wages at the source. The imposition of this tax seemed to be a general signal for the demand on the part of labor for increases in wages to offset the higher taxes, possibly because its impact was immediately felt due to deduction of the tax at the source. There is no doubt that the tax argument was used very extensively, and at a time when the tax was relatively insignificant as compared with present levels. Some may argue that the mere asking for higher wages to offset a new tax should not bring results in the absence of a real labor shortage, but I do not think this is sufficient answer. By the time taxes are sufficiently high to cut severely into accustomed standards of living the pressure for increased wages is bound to be extremely serious. If in addition to the very drastic individual income taxes there is in existence a tax approaching 100 per cent on excess profits there is a greatly lessened resistance on the part of employers to the urgent demands for more pay. It is true, of course, that employers may be reluctant to establish regimes of higher wage rates, but along with this reluctance there is also a strong desire to maintain peaceful relations in the plant.

To sum up at this point: Taxing to sop up surplus purchasing power and reduce the pull of consumer demand on prices in the absence of a wages ceiling may precipitate a movement resulting in a push on the cost side of the picture. After the price structure has been frozen there is still the danger that in taking the pressure off the commodity price structure you will dangerously add to the pressure on the wage and salary ceiling.

Canadian experience reveals another important limiting factor in the vigorous use of taxing power to curb inflation. I refer to the effect of high marginal tax rates on the incentive to work. It is said that high taxes are an important factor contributing to absenteeism and reluctance to work overtime. The advantage of moving from, say, low paid unnecessary work to higher paid important work may be very considerably reduced if taxes absorb too large a portion of the higher wages. These are very serious charges in wartime when maximum production, particularly in certain directions, is so vitally important. It is extremely difficult to know how much weight to attach to these charges. They have given us some concern in Canada.

We noted a quite high rate of absenteeism in certain directions in the United States at a time when no tax was being withheld there at the source. It was not easy to see that the absentee problem was worse in Canada with very high tax withholding than it was south of the line where there was no withholding. Furthermore, it is always to be expected that those receiving greater pay than they have been accustomed to are frequently disinclined to go after more money once they have enough in their pockets to meet immediate needs. The volume of adverse comment on the tax withholding system in Canada during the spring and summer of last year must, I think, be regarded as having drawn attention to a very real limiting point in a policy of heavy taxation.

Evaluation of Forced Savings

At this point I should comment on the use of the forced saving device in the tax structure. Forced saving or a refundable tax is a device which is appropriate, it seems to me, only after all possible adjustments have been forced in the taxpayer's current account position, and where the chief obstacle to further tax increases is found in the taxpayer's capital account. The main items in the capital account of the average taxpayer are savings commitments under insurance and annuity contracts, pension schemes and principal commitments on mortgages. Then, too, of course, there are past debts which the taxpayer is currently trying to pay out of income. It is at the point where the pressure of taxation has begun to impinge on voluntary savings commitments that the refundable tax or forced saving may appropriately be imposed with the privilege of offsetting against the tax these existing voluntary contractural savings commitments. It would be patently unfair to allow a person an exemption from a true tax merely because he has commitments under which he is building up an asset or reducing a capital liability. It is quite in order, however, to excuse him on these grounds from a general savings requirement which is enforced in the interests of price control.

In order to be worth the trouble the forced saving must produce a quite substantial sum of money. To get these worthwhile results the rates providing for the total take, that is, tax plus savings, must be very high. The inevitable result is high marginal rates of tax. This, then, brings me back to the point I mentioned a moment ago—the effect of these high marginal rates on production. Essentially the problem is that of deciding whether the benefits of withdrawing temporarily a certain fund of purchasing power from the pockets of a class of nonsavers is sufficient to outweigh the general deterrent effect on production over the *whole field* of taxpayers affected by the high marginal rates of tax. It may be argued that the taxpayer will realize that a portion of the amount taken from him through the high tax rates will be handed back to him and that in reality he is building up a savings fund for a rainy day. Logically this should be a perfect answer to the situation. The fact is, however, that ordinarily the worker discounts very substantially the value of this savings fund which is being built up on his account. This discounting can be corrected to some extent by showing the worker on each pay day how much of his deduction is true tax and how much is refundable. This, however, is a difficult requirement to impose on all employers. Many have voluntarily adopted the practice of showing the facts on the workers' pay envelopes. It is extremely important, however, in considering the value of the forced saving device that this discounting factor should be realized and considered in conjunction with the deterrent effects on production of the high rates of tax necessary to produce significant results.

Incomes Escaping Taxation

After having raised taxes up to the point where the wages ceiling is in jeopardy or the incentive to work is seriously impaired, there are still many fields in which the tax instrument cannot effectively reach incomes which properly should make a contribution to the Treasury. In the first place, almost all of us agree that there is some level of income below which, in the interests of health and decency, we should not tax. In arriving at this standard of exempt income it is usual to consider, for example, the young girl living in a city away from home. Only the very hardhearted would say she could decently get along on something less than $500, $600, or $700 a year, but in freeing her from tax on this much income we also free from tax all the youngsters who earn this much while living at home. They could easily pay a very heavy tax. This group of younger people who, as a rule, are free spenders, draw a very substantial fund of purchasing power which inevitably escapes the income tax net.

Agriculturists as a group—and they are a very large group in Canada—are not very effectively reached under an income tax. Accounting in this field is naturally very difficult and it might be said that taxable income is more often a matter of opinion rather than of fact.

Countless sole proprietors retailing goods and services, keeping no books and living out of the till, receive a very substantial total amount of income that may go tax-free, particularly when taxes, even in the lowest bracket, take at least 37 per cent.

These are some examples of cases representing in the aggregate a large volume of income which is difficult to reach under income tax. The result is that taxes have to be higher on the remainder of the community to secure the desired revenue.

Conclusion

In summary, the significant conclusion that emerges from Canadian experience is the fact that taxation *by itself* can never be an effective means of curbing inflation. Direct action in freezing the price and wage structure must be regarded as the main bulwark. Heavy taxation must be imposed right up to the danger points, however, to preserve the existence of the price ceiling, and to minimize the number of commodities which it is necessary to ration.

I think the essential achievement of our taxing policy was quite simply summed up in a conversation I overheard in a bus the other day. One fellow was telling another where he might go and how to proceed to buy a certain article and added "of course you'll have to expect to be soaked on the price." The reply was: "Thanks just the same. Not interested –I *can't afford it.*"

CHAPTER XVI

ENGLAND'S EXPERIENCE IN CURBING INFLATION THROUGH FISCAL DEVICES

MARY E. MURPHY

Hunter College of the City of New York

FEW ECONOMISTS in 1939 would have been so bold as to predict that the wartime increase in the British national income would reach its present high mark while, at the same time, the degree of price inflation was held at its current low level.

This course of events is a tribute to the demonstrated capacities and latent potentialities of the British financial structure. Not only has the Treasury mobilized the country for total war but, in addition, it has closed the inflationary gap by stabilizing prices and wages, rationing food and clothing, and siphoning off excess purchasing power at the source by the imposition of taxes and the encouragement of savings.

It cannot be claimed, of course, that inflation has not appeared in Britain at some stage in this war. When there was a wide margin for higher taxes and more stringent restrictions it was correct for the Treasury to press for these reforms and to preach the perils of inflation. But the limit has been reached and it is sufficient to state that the degree of inflation has been kept small, under control, and diverted to the less important sectors of the national economy.

Although finance has held the role of an instrument, not an arbiter, in wartime Britain the government has obtained funds on a scale never previously attained to pay for the fighting services, to subsidize civilian necessities, and to provide social security. The late Sir Kingsley Wood, in his post of Chancellor of the Exchequer, carried forward what he picturesquely described as the "battle of the damned noughts" by proposing one staggering war budget after another. These budgets were accepted by Parliament without a ripple of argument, a testimonial to the management of the national finances and to the readiness of the people to accept their fiscal punishment without complaint. For the first time in Britain, and perhaps in any other country, wartime finance has been related to the wider ramifications of economic and social policy, and not regarded as an independent procedure. The description and analysis of British financial policy in relation to the control of inflationary tendencies, with which this paper is concerned, are based on data furnished by government ministries and departments.[1] All conversions have been made at the rate of four dollars to a pound.

National Income

Under the impetus of war the national income in Britain has risen from $18 billion in 1938-39 to $23 billion in 1940-41, and finally to $24.8 billion in 1941-42. Government revenues, as a percentage of the national income, at those dates were 27.8 per cent, 31.2 per cent and 37.3 per cent, respectively; government expenditures, expressed in percentages at the same dates, were 30.9 per cent, 58.8 per cent and 67.4 per cent, respectively. War expenditure percentages of the national income, during this same period, rose from

[1] Statistical data have been compiled from Financial Statements prepared by the Chancellor of the Exchequer for the years 1938-44 and from Command Documents 6261, 6347 and 6438 titled, An Analysis of the Sources of War Finance and An Estimate of the National Income and Expenditure, and covering the years 1938-42.

TABLE I

ESTIMATES OF NET NATIONAL INCOME AND EXPENDITURE IN 1938, 1940, 1941 AND 1942

(In Millions)

	1938	1940	1941	1942
National Income:				
Rent of land and buildings	$1,524	$1,556	$1,540	$1,536
Profits and interest	4,964	6,496	7,704	8,732
Salaries, and the pay and allowances (in cash and kind) of officers in H. M. Forces and Auxiliary Services	4,324	5,152	5,352	5,632
Wages, and the pay and allowances (in cash and kind) of other ranks in H. M. Forces and Auxiliary Services	7,148	9,700	11,880	13,636
Net national income	$17,960	$22,904	$26,476	$29,536
National Expenditure:				
Personal expenditure on consumption at market prices	$16,140	$17,128	$18,036	$19,200
Expenditure at home and abroad, by public authorities, on goods and services at market prices	3,380	12,236	16,776	18,432
Private net investment at home and war losses made good	1,148	(−88)	(−800)	(−692)
Private and government net investment abroad	−220	−3,024	−3,188	−2,528
Subsidies	60	280	568	600
Less				
Indirect taxes and rates specifically on consumption	−1,724	−2,312	−3,080	−3,724
Other indirect taxes, rates, etc.	− 824	− 820	− 880	− 956
War risks insurance premiums	......	− 496	− 956	− 796
Net national expenditure	$17,960	$22,904	$26,476	$29,536

8.7 per cent to 42.1 per cent to 50.5 per cent. Between 1938 and 1942 increased national expenditure absorbed manpower and material resources equal to 55 per cent of the total national income and it was covered to the extent of 12½ per cent by increased output, 28½ per cent by demands on capital, and 14 per cent by reduced consumption.

Estimates of the net national income and expenditure in 1938, 1940, 1941, and 1942 are shown by the table on page 203.

Sources of War Finance

Government expenditures have risen from $4,084,000,000 in 1938-39 to an estimated $23,024,000,000 in 1943-44. Revenues at those same dates were $3,564,000,000 and $11,632,000,000, respectively. The sources of government finance from 1938 to the budget estimates for 1943-44 are shown in the table on page 205.

From every viewpoint these data indicate the excellent position of British war finance. Although total government expenditures have risen steadily during the period 1938-44, as shown by the foregoing tabulation, an increasing proportion of this outlay has been covered by revenue of which direct taxation has contributed a rising share. The increase in savings, in addition, has more than kept pace with the rise in budgetary deficits, while the share covered by capital disinvestment, both domestic and foreign, has decreased.

For the entire period from September, 1939, to April, 1942, government expenditures were financed 43 per cent by taxation, 35 per cent by loans, and 22 per cent by floating debt. In the fiscal year 1943-44 the Treasury expects that revenue will provide 50.5 per cent of the total expenditure (56.4 per cent of the expenditure requiring domestic finance) compared with 52 per cent in 1942 and 48 per cent in 1941. A comparison of the record of this war with that of the last indicates that finance has been placed on a much more stable basis as, in the twelve months ended on October 31, 1918, only 29 per cent of the total expenditure was covered by revenue with the major portion of the borrowing raised at

TABLE II

SOURCES OF GOVERNMENT FINANCE IN 1938, 1940, 1941, 1942 AND THE BUDGET FORECAST FOR 1943-44
(In Millions)

	1938	1940	1941	1942	Budget Forecast 1943–44
Central government revenue:					
Direct taxation on personal incomes, including death duties, etc.	$1,680	$2,248	$2,968	$3,400	$7,496
Direct taxation on non-personal incomes	308	688	1,388	2,160	
Indirect taxation	1,488	2,008	2,820	2,532	4,000
Miscellaneous income	88	92	136	280	136
Total central government revenue	$3,564	$5,036	$7,312	$9,372	$11,632
Savings:					
Personal savings (net)	$536	$2,512	$2,816	$3,564	.....
Non-personal savings (net)	680	700	720	760	.....
Excess tax liabilities:					
Personal	68	376	824	1,120	.....
Non-personal	48	732	932	592	.....
Surplus of extra-budgetary funds and local authorities	116	744	880	924	.....
Compensation received for war damage claims	.....	144	992	860	.....
Total savings	$1,448	$5,208	$7,164	$7,820	.....
Capital disinvestment:					
Overseas disinvestment	$220	$3,024	$3,188	$2,528	.....
Residue, being the net disinvestment of capital at home	−1,148	88	800	692	.....
Total Capital disinvestment	−928	3,112	3,988	3,220	.....
Total central government expenditure	$4,084	$13,356	$18,464	$20,412	$23,024

rates well over double those prevailing at the present time.

The Chancellor of the Exchequer has continued to warn that although the national accounts will always balance it is only in the case they are balanced in other ways than by taxation, combined with other Treasury aids and resources and genuine savings, that the danger of inflation will arise. Treasury policy has been coordinated with that of other government departments to reduce consumption to the level required by existing supplies of consumers' goods and to influence citizens in the use of their incomes. The direct methods have included rationing consumers' goods and limiting their output by the establishment of production quotas, and the concentration of nonessential industries; indirect procedures have consisted of price control, taxation, and savings campaigns. These controls increased in scope and severity with the expansion in note circulation and in volume of bank deposits, and with the increase of salaries, wages, and overtime payments. Any inflationary tendency in the months that lie ahead between war and peace will be reflected not by a price rise but, instead, by an increasingly wide extension of rationing and of restrictions to the use of money.

The real sources of war finance in the years 1940, 1941, and 1942 are shown in the following tabulation.[2]

It is apparent from these data that there has been a steady increase in the proportion of war expenditure covered by current sources, that is, by increased production, and a constant decrease of other sources. While the portion provided by reduced consumption remained at about 25 per cent, the share furnished by increased output rose from 17 per cent to 43 per cent between 1940 and 1942, and the amount derived

[2] Kaldor, Nicholas, "The 1943 White Paper on National Income and Expenditure," *Economic Journal,* June-Sept., 1943, pp. 259-74.

by reduced domestic and foreign investment declined from 60 per cent to 32 per cent in the same period.

TABLE III

REAL SOURCES OF WAR FINANCE IN 1940, 1941 AND 1942
(In Millions at 1938 Prices)

	1940	1941	1942
Increase in output	$1,200	$2,840	$4,560
Reduction in consumption	1,660	2,580	2,660
Increase in adverse overseas balance	1,820	1,780	1,140
Reduction in private investment, including the reduction of stocks in private ownership	2,500	2,460	2,260
Increase in government expenditure on goods and services, as compared with 1938	$7,180	$9,660	$10,620

Personal expenditure on consumption, after adjustment for subsidies and indirect taxes, is estimated to have changed as follows between 1938 and 1942.

TABLE IV

PERSONAL EXPENDITURE ON CONSUMPTION AT MARKET PRICES IN 1938, 1940, 1941 AND 1942
(In Millions)

	1938	1940	1941	1942
Personal expenditure on consumption at market prices	$16,140	$17,128	$18,036	$19,200
Plus subsidies	60	280	568	600
	$16,200	$17,408	$18,604	$19,800
Less indirect taxes specifically on consumption	1,724	2,312	3,080	3,724
Personal consumption thus adjusted	$14,476	$15,096	$15,524	$16,076

Government estimates of the movements in real consumption are based on an inquiry into the change of retail prices covering approximately 90 per cent of the total of civilian expenditure on consumption. They indicate that retail prices, when specific indirect taxes on consumption have been deducted and subsidies added, have risen by 18 per cent, 30 per cent and 36 per cent in 1940, 1941 and 1942, respectively, while the reduction in aggregate real consumption, at the same dates, totaled 12 per cent, 18 per cent and 18 per cent. The constancy of the total level of consumption in 1941 and 1942 is rather surprising, especially when it is remembered that various new means of restriction, including clothes rationing, had been introduced in the latter year. It is explained, however, by the facts that more than half of the total expenditure was on food, rent, fuel, and light, that no proper account was taken of reductions of quality, and that the figures include lend-lease deliveries for civilian consumption which were appreciably higher in 1942 than in 1941.

Indexes of retail sales of the Bank of England, based upon 1937 as 100, have risen from 105 for food and perishables for the twelve months ending June 30, 1939, to 114 at June 30, 1943, but the indexes of other goods, at the same dates, have declined from 101 to 97, with the downward movement in the turnover of goods accelerated during 1943.

Price Control

The achievement of complete price stability in Britain was rendered impossible by the depreciation of the pound at the outbreak of hostilities and the consequent rise in the cost of imports. Compared with the last war, however, price rises have been much less marked and price control has proved much more successful in moderating inflation.

Government price control policy, initiated in September, 1939, has been experimental rather than systematic, with emphasis placed upon restraining increases of spendable incomes, limiting private expenditure, and proposing specific action to hold key points in the price structure. It has limited the expansion in the volume of incomes in the hands of the public and business firms by restricting, but not entirely prohibiting, rises in wage rates and dividends, and by drastically increasing personal and business taxes and direct levies on nonessential goods and services. On the other hand, nothing has been done to prohibit the rise in gross business profits although the excess above the prewar level has been brought within an excess profits tax. Wage rates have not been frozen at the prewar level, but their rise has been restrained by various devices, such as the stabilization of the official cost-of-living index in 1941 and the maintenance of the prewar machinery of collective bargaining reinforced by compulsory arbitration of disputes.

An examination of British price policy illustrates the close connection between general measures designed to limit the pressure of purchasing power upon a dwindling supply of goods and services, and devices designed to prevent, or slow down, the rise in the cost of specific groups of commodities and services. The combined effect of these two sets of measures is indicated by the following table.

TABLE V

PERSONAL INCOME AND OUTLAY IN 1938 AND 1942
(In Millions)

	1938	1942
Personal income	$18,644	$27,584
Spent on: Taxes	$3,632	$7,944
Savings	536	3,564
Consumption	14,476	16,076
	$18,644	$27,584

While the aggregate personal income, in the above tabulation, shows an increase of nearly 50 per cent, a substantial part of this rise, perhaps as much as two-fifths, may be attributed to higher production; the net increase in expenditure on consumption, totaling 11 per cent may, therefore, be considered to be comparatively small. In its own purchases the government, in the absence of peacetime competition, has relied on a carefully designed system of cost accounts with the aim of discouraging extravagance in the use of scarce resources and of encouraging personal initiative. In the control of the prices of goods purchased by the public, however, the government has steadily extended price control until it covers virtually all foods and essential personal and household goods. In order to implement its policy of stabilizing the official cost-of-living index the prices of many foodstuffs have been subsidized, but essential commodities are normally sold to the consumer on a cost basis. Luxuries, as well as many items which can be termed "conventional necessities," have been permitted to find their own level with their prices, in actuality, increased by heavy indirect taxes.

The following table indicates that the general cost-of-living index has remained stable since April, 1941, and in the case

TABLE VI

COST-OF-LIVING INDEX

	Sept., 1939	April, 1941	Sept., 1943
All items	100	128	128
Food	100	123	120
Clothing	100	172	166
Rent	100	101	101
Fuel and light	100	124	134
Other items	100	126	163

of food, which accounts for nearly 50 per cent of the working-class budget, the rise has been proportionately small compared with other items.

The rise of 28 per cent in the cost of living from September, 1939, to September, 1943, of which 2.9 per cent is due to increased taxes on sugar and tobacco and about 0.8 per cent to the purchase tax, contrasts with the increase of 90 per cent in the index during a comparable period of the last war. Food prices alone, as can be seen from the foregoing tabulation, rose by only 20 per cent to September, 1943, as compared with 108 per cent in the period from 1914 to 1918. The government's policy of subsidizing clothing, transport and essential foodstuffs, now costing $800,000,000 annually, has materially reduced the cost of staple foods to the consumer and has raised the nutritional standards of lower-income groups. As a general rule, subsidies are not granted or taxes remitted until an effective control of prices, and in most cases of supply, has been attained. For example, there has been no general remission of the purchase tax on clothing although utility clothes, which unlike other wearing apparel are manufactured under the close supervision of the Board of Trade, have been made free of the purchase tax.

The objects of price and subsidy policy include not only the stabilization of the cost-of-living index but, in conjunction with measures of rationing and distribution control, the provision of adequate supplies of essential articles to all sections of the community. No single government ministry or measure has been permitted to rule the scene but a concerted advance in the imposition of checks and balances has provided such an admirable system of price control that living costs have ceased to be a working-class problem.[3]

---

[3] For a detailed description of price control see British Information Services Pamphlet No. 312, November, 1943.

Wage Control

The conversion of the economy to a war basis was accompanied by powerful inflationary forces in the form of increased earnings of previously unemployed workers and of rising wages and overtime rates in the munitions industries. Unemployment has become virtually nonexistent as out of 33,000,000 citizens between the ages of 14 and 64 nearly 23,000,000 have entered paid occupation in the armed services, Civil Defense, war industries, and essential occupations. The great expansion of lower-bracket incomes is apparent from an estimate made in July, 1942, which revealed that the number of individuals earning $500-$2,000 a year increased from 9,000,000 in 1938-39 to 12,700,000 in 1941-42.

The Ministry of Labour's average rates of wages for the usual working week rose by only 26½ per cent between October, 1938, and January, 1943, but average earnings advanced by 65 per cent during the same period. The disparity between these two figures is due to the longer hours worked, the movement of workers from low-paid jobs into the more remunerative war industries, and the increase in the output of labor on piece rates. A large portion of the advance in weekly earnings has been caused by factors which would have operated even if wage rates had been frozen at prewar levels, and earnings, in contrast to profits, have been permitted to remain as an incentive to increased output.

At the inception of war, the government agreed to respect the voluntary machinery of collective negotiation between organized workers and organized employers as the method of determining wages. In July, 1941, the official document, *Price Stabilization and Industrial Policy,* Cmd. 6294, was issued in which it was stated that every effort would be made to avoid modification of this machinery, and that the cost-of-living index number, apart from minor seasonal changes, was to be held within the range of 125-130 in terms of the prewar level. The government argued that, as the cost of living was to be stabilized, there should be no need for workers to press for further increases in basic wage rates except for the purpose of leveling-up low rates.

The Trade Union Congress, however, did not fully accept this view and urged the government to rely on control of selling prices, extension of the rationing system, and provision of subsidies at the source to lower the cost to the consumer of certain essential commodities, and on taxation and savings to stave off inflation. All these items were accepted as part of the government's policy and they have been extended from time to time as, for example, by taxation of wages at the source.

In practice, some wage increases requested by unions have been granted while others have been refused. In considering cases the National Arbitration Tribunal, a wartime body capable of making binding decisions, bears the general stabilization position constantly in mind. Recent changes in wage rates have occurred in industries in which the wartime rise had been less than the average, with the general intention observed of bringing the lowest time-rate for the normal week up to a minimum standard without raising higher wages proportionately. Even with a more liberal interpretation of the increase of prices, including those which do not affect the index, it is clear that the average real earnings are considerably higher in 1944 than in 1939, in most cases even after deducting income taxes.

The stabilization policy and the wage policy of the government may be considered to be complementary with the former depending upon the latter and obviating the necessity of increases of wages where automatic adjustments are linked to the cost-of-living figure. In practice, average increases in wage rates have been larger than the increases in retail prices shown by the cost-of-living index, with the index of necessities actually far below the net increases in earnings. The wartime wage policy, just described, has proved of material aid in maintaining the sense of responsibility and self-government which has characterized British business for many years, and it has fostered the industrial peace essential to the promotion of the war effort.

Taxation

As the stabilization of wages, in the face of increased employment and decreased supplies of consumers' goods, could not entirely prevent the rise of prices the government was forced to draw off excess purchasing power by taxation and by savings. In the pursuit of a coordinated tax program the Treasury has raised the income tax to a standard rate of 50 per cent which, plus surtax, means that the total tax on all incomes over $80,000 is 97½ per cent.[4] Allowances have been reduced and assessment now starts for a single person at $440 a year.

Since the highest incomes were already heavily taxed before the war, the most striking increase in tax yield has come from the greatly enlarged $500-$2,000 a year income group. In 1938-39 this group paid $92,000,000 in taxes while in 1942-43 the amount had risen to $1,100,000,000. The increase in both the number of taxpayers and the amount of tax paid is apparent from these data: In 1939 1,000,000 week-

[4] The standard rate of income tax in 1937-38 was 25 per cent, in April, 1938, 27½ per cent, in September, 1939, 35 per cent, in April, 1940, 37½ per cent, in September, 1940, 42½ per cent, and in April, 1941, 50 per cent. From 1931-38 surtax began on all incomes over $8,000 a year at the rate of 5½ per cent rising to a maximum of 41¼ per cent on incomes over $200,000. In 1938-39 the initial rate rose to 6½ per cent and the maximum to 47½ per cent on all incomes over $120,000. In April, 1939, the initial rate rose to 10 per cent and the figure over which the maximum of 47½ per cent was paid was reduced to $80,000.

ly wage earners paid $10,000,000 in income taxes; in 1943 7,000,000 paid $800,000,000. In spite of the fact that lower-income groups have been called upon to make a much heavier contribution in the form of direct taxes, the instrument of taxation has accentuated the redistribution of gross incomes in their favor. At the present time 10,000,000 out of 12,500,000 taxpayers belong to these groups. In the $2,000-$4,000 group, in fact, increases in gross income have been virtually wiped out by taxation, and the aggregate net income in the group over $4,000 has been substantially reduced.

In the latest year for which figures are available, namely

TABLE VII

DISTRIBUTION OF PRIVATE INCOME BY RANGES OF GROSS INCOME SHOWING THE EFFECT OF CHANGES IN INCOME TAX AND SURTAX

Financial year 1941-42

	Number of Incomes (In thousands)	Aggregate Gross Income 1941–42 (In millions)	Aggregate Net Income with Income Tax and Surtax at		Proportion of Gross Income Retained with Taxes at	
			1938–39 Rates	1941–42 Rates	1938–39 Rates	1941–42 Rates
			(In millions)		(In percentages)	
Private income at the disposal of individuals:						
Under $1,000....	.....	$13,592	$13,568	$13,228	99.8	97.3
$ 1,000-$ 2,000..	4,450	5,960	5,780	5,104	97.0	85.6
$ 2,000-$ 4,000..	1,050	2,740	2,452	1,980	89.5	72.3
$ 4,000-$ 8,000..	285	1,600	1,312	980	82.0	61.3
$ 8,000-$40,000..	97	1,440	1,024	680	71.1	47.2
$40,000 & over...	8	680	336	140	49.4	20.6
Other private income.	.....	$3,044	.....	$800	....	26.3
Total private income..	.....	$29,056	.....	$22,912	....	78.9

1941-42, the 8,000 persons who received $40,000 a year or more retained on the average 20.6 per cent of their original incomes after they had paid their taxes, while the 4,450,000 persons in the $1,000-$2,000 income range retained 85.6 per cent of their incomes. These facts are apparent from a perusal of the table on page 215.

In 1941-42 the income tax and surtax raised $1,180,000,000 from incomes below $2,000 a year and $2,500,000,000 from incomes of $2,000 and over. Persons earning $2,000 in 1938-39 paid 7.9 per cent of total British taxes and in 1941-42 32.4 per cent, while those earning over $8,000 paid 64 per cent and 38.9 per cent at those dates. The proportion of private income devoted to taxation in the years 1938-42 is shown by the following table.

TABLE VIII

PROPORTION OF PRIVATE INCOME DEVOTED TO TAXATION 1938-42
(In Millions)

	1938	1940	1941	1942
Private income	$19,680	$24,624	$28,252	$31,344
Direct taxes, social insurance contributions of employees, War Damage Act contributions and premiums met out of private income	$2,208	$3,176	$4,924	$6,108
Indirect taxes and rates specifically on consumption, less subsidies	1,664	2,032	2,512	3,124
Other indirect taxes, etc., met out of private income	680	800	960	880
Excess of tax liabilities in respect of private income	116	1,108	1,756	1,712
Total tax liabilities	$4,668	$7,116	$10,152	$11,824
Total tax liabilities as a percentage of national income	24%	29%	36%	38%

A form of compulsory savings was introduced during the financial year ending March 31, 1942, under which, instead of imposing a separate levy for compulsory savings on incomes, part of the increase in personal taxation was earmarked for this purpose. The proportion of the income tax credited to the individual was shown on a graduated scale; in the lowest income groups it totaled 100 per cent but the amount declined sharply as the tax payable rose. The amount of credit depended upon the size of the taxpayer's income, his marital status, and whether his income was earned or derived from investments. The credit was subject to a maximum of $240 a year for a single person and $260 for a married couple as to earned income, and $40 and $60, respectively, for investment income.

A pay-as-you-go system of income tax collection was adopted in the fall of 1943 under which, beginning with April 6, 1944, weekly wage earners will pay their tax on the basis of current weekly earnings.[5] The novelty of the system lies in what is called the "cumulative tax" principle. Instead of trying to calculate separately the tax on each pay envelope, the tax is calculated and withheld on the basis of the wage earner's total earnings in the financial year up to and including that pay period. In this calculation the exact amount of personal tax reliefs for the same pay period is automatically taken into account by means of a simple tax table. The amount of tax deducted by the employer from every pay envelope is the total tax due on the aggregate earnings up to and including that pay period, less, the tax already deducted in the previous pay periods of the financial year. For example, a married man with one child entitled to deduct $760 would fall under Code 33. If his gross pay amounted to $39.20 in

[5] Explained in *A New System for the Taxation of the Weekly Wage Earners*, Cmd. 6469, September, 1943.

the first week, he would be taxed to the extent of $7.60, of which $7.60 would be deducted. If the gross pay amounted to $38.00 in the second week, the total tax due for the two weeks would be $13.40, of which $5.80 would be deducted. The respective figures for the third week would be $35.20, $20.20, and $6.80, and for the fourth week $36.40, $27.00, and $6.80. That is, the four weekly tax deductions would be exactly equal to the total tax liability of $27.00 for the four weeks.

The great advantage of this new system is that, when it is in operation, no adjustments will be required at the end of the year if a wage earner, receiving large sums at one period, does not maintain this level of earnings during the rest of the year. The adjustments take place automatically with each tax payment, and at the end of the year every wage earner is "straight" with the income tax authorities. This tax method was devised by the Treasury to meet the problem, common to every country engaged in a war, of the time lag in the tax payments of a vastly increased number of taxpayers. Attempts had been made to meet this problem in 1940 by introducing deduction of tax at the source for all wage and salary earners, but the amount subtracted by the employer from every salary check and pay envelope was still calculated on the basis of the earnings in a previous period. The new system was so enthusiastically received that it has been extended to include salary earners up to $2,400 a year with the Treasury promising its further extension, with safeguards, to all salary earners.

A purchase tax was put in operation in October, 1940, for the first time in British history. At the present time it imposes levies ranging from 16 2/3 per cent to 33 1/3 per cent on articles of common use with 100 per cent assessed on luxuries.[6] This tax does not apply to food or utility goods, or to beer, tobacco, whiskey, sugar, and tea which are subject to special excise taxes. It is collected at the wholesale level and passed on to retailers and consumers. The purpose of the different rates is to introduce the progressive principle into the purchase tax. Essential items, representing the bulk of the spending of lower-income groups, are either exempt or covered by the lowest levies, while less essential goods bear a very heavy tax.

The following table shows the steep rise in various types of taxation derived by the central government from 1938-39 to the budget estimate of 1943-44.

TABLE IX

CENTRAL GOVERNMENT TAXATION
(In Millions)

	1938–39	1942–43	1943–44 (Est.)
Income tax and surtax	$1,592	$4,328	$5,020
Excess profits tax	88	1,510	2,000
Indirect taxes	1,364	3,540	3,902
Other revenue	540	552	572
Total revenue from taxes	$3,584	$9,930	$11,494

Budget estimates of taxation for the year 1943-1944 represent about $160 per capita for direct taxation and about $80 per capita for indirect taxation. Indirect taxes, which are proportionately a heavier burden on low, rather than on high, incomes, have risen steadily so that, at the present time, a pint of beer costs 20c of which 11c is tax and a package of cigarettes costs 46c of which 35c is tax. Estate duties rise

[6] The tax was imposed in 1940 at the rate of 33 1/3 per cent on luxuries and 16 2/3 per cent on other goods. In April, 1942, the levy on luxury articles was raised to 66 2/3 per cent and in April, 1943, to 100 per cent.

from 1 per cent on an estate of $400, to 36 per cent on one valued at $1,000,000, and to 65 per cent on an $8,000,000 estate. The tax program, in addition, includes stamp and other inland revenue duties, customs duties and motor vehicle duties; local taxes levied by local authorities on all occupied property; social security payments, required of all manual workers and non-manual workers earning up to $2,500 a year, to National Unemployment and Health Insurance Funds; and war damage and war risk premiums made under the War Damage Act and the Marine and Commodity War Risk Insurance Schemes. An excess profits tax was levied at the rate of 60 per cent to April, 1940, and then raised to 100 per cent with a refund of 20 per cent promised after the war.[7] As an alternative to this tax a national defense contribution, that is, a tax on profits at the rate of 5 per cent for a corporation and 4 per cent for an unincorporated business, is paid if it is found to yield more.

It has been calculated that an average married man, with two dependent children, earning $1,200 a year pays only $39 in income tax but his total tax and compulsory payments amount to $252 or 21.2 per cent of his income. The same man earning $4,000 pays $1,200 in income tax and a total of $1,600 (or 40 per cent) in all his tax and compulsory levies. With income taxes at the present rate, 85 per cent of the net purchasing power of Britain remains in the hands of citizens with gross incomes under $2,000 a year. The Treasury has benefited from the facts that the revenue bill and the budget are part of the same piece of legislation, that tax regulations and forms are constantly simplified and improved, and that the public and the accounting profession are deemed capable of carrying the tax laws into effect. The British tax system has

[7] For calculation of this tax see British Information Services Pamphlet No. 236, November, 1943.

proved highly satisfactory in raising a higher proportion of revenue than in any previous war, controlling current purchasing power and inflationary price rises, providing amounts which when peace comes can be paid to counteract the post-war slump, and securing far-reaching social reforms including the conception of the national minimum.

Voluntary Savings

Although the last war fostered a wave of spending it may be stated that this conflict has stimulated a wave of saving among all sections of the community. By September, 1943, in fact, large and small savers had contributed more than $25 billion to the Treasury, an average of $537 per head of population. Total war savings, however, do not provide an accurate picture of genuine savings out of income since they arise, in the main, from capital sources. It is interesting to note, therefore, that the total raised in small savings totaled more than $9 billion by September, 1943, an average of $195 per person, compared with $1.096 billion, or $24.80 per capita for the period 1916-18.

Although the amount secured in taxation is definite, the amount spent under the heading of personal expenditure is not. Appeals for loans, therefore, have to be directed to a fluid and indeterminate portion of the individual's income. No compulsion has been placed on a person to invest in a government loan but the field for other types of investment is limited as only securities quoted in sterling can be purchased and every transaction must be on a cash basis.

Summary

While the money income of Britain has steadily increased under the stimulus of war, taxation and savings have proved eminently successful in checking a simultaneous increase in net spending power. This program to limit spending has been complementary to rationing, with price control assuming its proper place as a means of maintaining economic and social stability in spite of the vastly expanded war effort and the severely contracted supply of consumers' goods. Although the government has achieved a unique record in warding off inflation the struggle is not over, as an appreciable expansion in earnings might give rise to sufficient pressure on costs and prices to upset the equilibrium.

As postwar problems emerge it is apparent that the redirection of manpower and material resources to the purposes of peace, the financing of reconstruction at low rates of interest, and the maintenance of balance between the supply of consumers' goods and the purchasing power of the community will necessitate the continuance of economic control. If the Treasury's financial plans, designed to ease the difficult path between war and peace, incorporate the continuance of rationing and price control until supplies are sufficient to prevent an inflationary price rise, and also continue the judicious use of the taxing power and the encouragement of the savings movement, the British people will have little to fear from the scourge of inflation.

PART FIVE

POSSIBILITIES OF POSTWAR INFLATION AND SUGGESTED TAX ACTION

CHAPTER XVII

POSSIBILITIES OF POSTWAR INFLATION AND SUGGESTED TAX ACTION

Marriner S. Eccles

Chairman, Board of Governors, Federal Reserve System

A discussion of taxation from the standpoint of controlling *inflation* in the postwar period would be incomplete unless account is also taken of the importance of taxation as a means of controlling *deflation*. Taxation is never neutral in its economic effects, and since the war, it has been more and more generally recognized that even if levied ostensibly for revenue only, taxes have a direct influence on those basic factors of consumption, savings, and investment which, by getting out of balance, produce economic ups and downs. It is appropriate to discuss these matters in this forum. It is important to consider what type and what amount of taxation will best help to keep the economy moving ahead on an even keel when the war ends and looking to the longer future.

At the same time, it is of paramount importance not to lose sight of the stark fact that we are still in the midst of this war. It is not yet won. No man can say when it will end. No man can say what it will cost in blood and resources before it ends. The imperative needs of this hour are more determined and united effort, more manpower, more taxation, and more restraints. If in the discussions of the postwar world—in the debates going on all over this country about postwar plans and problems—we blind ourselves or others to the urgent necessities of this war, if our will as a nation to exert every effort to achieve an early victory is in any way weakened by thinking too much about our dollars in the future and too little about our duties now, we shall have done our country, and ourselves, a grave disservice.

Proper fiscal policies are, of course, essential to the successful management of our war economy. They will be equally essential to a full utilization of our resources later on. In bringing the problems of fiscal policy before the public your Institute is making an important contribution towards the promotion of those policies which should contribute to the successful financing of this war and to the maintenance thereafter of the institutions which our armed forces are fighting to preserve.

War Finance and Postwar Inflation

Our home front fight against inflation will have to continue for a considerable time after the war ends. The eventual answer to the inflation problem must be found in the production of goods in quantities sufficient to meet all the demand, but that will not be possible until industry has been able to resume full peacetime production and has been able to supply the most urgent backlog needs. In the meantime we shall still be confronted with a situation in which individual and business consumers, if permitted to buy freely, would in many fields try to purchase greatly in excess of what is available. Thus the pressure on many prices will continue. In order to assure orderly transition to a high and stable level of production and employment in the postwar period, it is absolutely essential that further price increases be prevented. This cannot be done without maintaining wartime taxes, wage controls, and also rationing and price controls over essential goods, until such time as the supply is sufficient to meet demand. Also, control of goods for export should be maintained for some time.

I shall not undertake to restate my views on war finance, but in discussing the problems of inflation control after the war, we must realize that the chances for success at that time will be vitally affected by fiscal policies during the war. Our tax effort so far has been entirely inadequate in relationship to our huge wartime expenditures and it has lagged far behind that of our allies. A family man with an income of $5,000, for instance, pays $754 of income taxes in the United States (including state income tax at the rate paid in New York State) as against $1,655 in the United Kingdom or $1,747 in Canada. Not only is the present level of income taxes much higher in these two countries, but the increase over prewar taxes has also been much sharper. In addition, the American pays considerably less in sales and excise taxes than does the taxpayer in either of the two other countries.

A few illustrations will show the relationship of the current war financing program to postwar developments. For every dollar of income currently received in the United States, less than 65 cents worth of consumers' goods are currently available for purchase, and for every dollar of disposable income which is left to the consumer after the payment of his personal taxes, there are less than 75 cents worth of goods that can be bought. Our failure to accept a substantial increase in taxes at this time thus leaves us with an excess of consumers' income which greatly increases the difficulties of effective rationing and of holding the line against further wage and price increases. We should strengthen in every way possible our stabilization program during the war period, since it will be impossible to do so after the war, when the impulse of the people to return to normalcy will make it very difficult even to maintain established controls.

Another difficulty which will confront us in the postwar period will arise from the huge amount of purchasing power held by the public. This will largely be the result of our heavy reliance upon borrowing in the financing of our war expenditures, and, in particular, upon borrowing from the banks. In the two years from January 1, 1942, to January 1, 1944, the public debt increased by 105 billion dollars, and of this increase the commercial banks and the Federal Reserve Banks have absorbed 48 billion dollars. Of the total of 169 billion dollars of interest-bearing United States Government securities outstanding at the end of 1943, 72 billion were held by the commercial banks and the Federal Reserve. This extensive borrowing from the banks resulted in a corresponding increase in our money supply. Including currency as well as demand deposits, the total money supply held by the public at the close of the year amounted to over 80 billion dollars, or nearly twice as much as two years ago. To this must be added over 30 billion dollars of time deposits and the many billions of United States Government securities held by the public. This huge volume of liquid funds is the basis for the inflationary problem in the transition period.

Problem of Postwar Transition

In turning our attention to the transition problem, we would do well to remember what happened after the last war. The collapse of Germany came unexpectedly. It was followed by an abrupt termination of war production. Prompt abandonment of price controls after the Armistice, record agricultural exports, heavy inventory accumulations and high consumers' demand led to the sharp price advances of 1919 and 1920, which, in turn, paved the way for the postwar depression. This time the transition problem will be immensely greater. War expenditures in 1918 amounted to only 16 billion dollars as against 90 billion dollars now. Then, only one-fourth of all goods produced by the economy were for war purposes; now, the war absorbs about one-half of our total output. We need to be far more successful this time in solving the problem. Early resumption of peacetime production by some industries, if properly planned, could help to remove bottlenecks in the reconversion of other industries later on. A gradual demobilization of the services would greatly reduce the danger of flooding the labor market in the earlier stages of reconversion. Should the Pacific war continue for some time after the fall of Germany, a more gradual tapering off of war production and demobilization of the armed forces would, of course, be possible than would be the case if the Axis were to collapse simultaneously on all fronts.

But, we cannot depend upon the Axis to time its collapse to suit our economic convenience. Rather, we must prepare for the most speedy return of industry to peacetime production whenever military requirements permit. We must stand ready to meet inflationary pressures while this shift is being accomplished. A speedy conversion to peacetime production is the most direct and effective way to cope with the inflation problem. On industry's part, this requires advance planning for the return to an expanded production so that a high level of employment can be maintained with the least possible interruption. It is important that the expansion of industry should be only in those fields where it is justified by the promise of a permanent market. Expansion should be avoided where it would merely serve to meet a temporary high level of demand arising from the huge backlog of deferred purchases. This backlog should be met gradually. Otherwise, excess capacity while being created would accentuate the inflation danger during the transition period and the danger of deflation later on.

On the government's part, an orderly and expeditious transition requires the setting up of effective machinery for the prompt termination and payment of amounts due on outstanding contracts, for the disposition of inventories and government-owned facilities needed in peacetime production and for assuring an ample credit supply. If claims against outstanding government contracts are settled promptly, the credit position of business on the whole will be very strong. There are a few large enterprises and many small businesses, however, which will be in need of funds, either in the form of credit, equity capital, or both. All necessary steps should be taken to assure that these needs will be met. The funds should be supplied as far as possible from private sources with such government assistance as may be required.

Even though we may succeed in resuming peacetime production rapidly, there will still be a period of heavy inflationary pressures due to the desire of consumers to satisfy their deferred demands, and the requirements of business for supplies to take care of deferred maintenance and improvements and to restock inventories. Heavy export demands will also continue. It is most important that prices be held from the outset and that the public be confident of this policy. We must give assurance to the millions of bondholders that they will not lose by delaying their purchases until ample supplies are again available. If wartime savings are used gradually after industry has returned to a peacetime basis, they can contribute greatly to the maintenance of prosperity. But if spent too rapidly, the savings would be dissipated in higher prices and would undermine the foundations of the economy.

There can be no doubt, therefore, that inflation controls should be maintained during this transition period. Continued rationing and price controls will be needed in the domestic market, and licensing control of exports should be retained. Wartime taxes should be kept up, including the excess profits tax, although it may be desirable to reduce the present 95 per cent rate to, say, 75 per cent, in order to encourage efficiency, economy and increased production. The drastic reduction of expenditures which will take place will not justify a premature reduction of taxes. On the contrary, every attempt should be made to bring about a balanced budget at the earliest possible date after the war. It is unlikely that the public will be absorbing additional government securities during that period, but will be tending to sell on balance some of its holdings. Unless the budget is balanced, the banks would not only have to absorb possible sales by nonbank holders, but would also have to absorb the new issues needed to finance the deficit, thus aggravating the inflationary situation by further increasing the already excessive supply of money. A balanced budget, on the other hand, will encourage the owners of government bonds to retain their holdings because it will assure them that the purchasing power of their money, invested in bonds, will be preserved.

Task of Maintaining Production in Peacetime

After the war is won and industry has been fully readjusted to a peacetime basis, American enterprise will meet its greatest challenge, namely, to provide peacetime production on a scale commensurate with the enormous ability to produce which our economy has demonstrated during the war years. This will mean the employment of at least 55 million people, as compared with 46 million in 1940, when more people were employed than in any previous year. At 1943 prices, this means a gross national product of about 160 billion dollars, or close to 45 billion dollars more than in 1940.

To meet this challenge, we must realize that a high level

of employment and income requires a high level of expenditures, private or public. We have seen during the war years how greatly our national product can be increased if there is sufficient demand for the country's output. After the transition has been made, we shall be able to maintain a high level of output only if a vast increase in peacetime expenditures replaces a large part of the war outlays. Business will not be able to supply a product of 160 billion dollars unless there is a corresponding demand by the economy as a whole. Demand will not be sufficient unless business distributes its income to the people, and unless the people return their incomes to enterprise in the purchase of its goods and services. This means, first of all, maintenance of a high volume of wages. The aggregate of buying power must be maintained, although some wages may have to be adjusted downward and others upward. This buying power must then be returned to the economy through a high level of consumption expenditures. Of course, not all income will be spent on consumption. There will be savings both by individuals and by business enterprises. We can have saving and a high level of income and employment if the savings are invested in the improvement and expansion of our economy. When savings are thus spent upon the production of new facilities of all kinds, they provide income and employment. But when savings are held idle, or used to bid up the prices of existing assets, they are not returned to production and other dollars must take their place if employment is to be maintained. The basic condition for economic prosperity is thus a steady stream of consumer, business, and public expenditures at a volume sufficient to employ all who desire to work. The more fully private enterprise succeeds in providing the necessary volume of income and expenditures, the less necessary it will be for government—federal, state and local—to provide supplementary employment.

Postwar Tax Policies

The contribution which monetary policy can make to the goal of maximum production and employment is limited. The banking system and the capital market must provide adequate funds to meet the credit and capital needs of the country. Merely making funds available, however low the cost, will not induce expansion unless business is assured of a market for its increased production. On the other hand, the impact of fiscal policies on the spending stream is far more direct and powerful. Revenue measures and public expenditures can either increase or decrease the income stream. The government can so shape and time its tax and expenditure policies as to offset variations in the income stream due to variations in the volume of private expenditures. By wise policy, correctly timed, government can thus be a balance wheel and a stabilizing influence in helping to maintain a high level of production and employment. Taxation, therefore, has become much more than a problem merely of meeting the fiscal needs of the Treasury. It is also a major concern of national economic policy.

There is much discussion currently about incentive taxation, as if it were a panacea. Every taxpayer, individual or corporate, is inclined to think that the best incentive would be to reduce *his own* taxes. Thus, the argument for tax incentives readily develops into an argument for greatly reduced taxes for everybody. Greatly reducing everybody's taxes, however, is not the way to maintain a balanced budget, as we certainly should do when we have a high level of peacetime employment. It is likely that the federal postwar budget will be well above 20 billion dollars annually. Therefore, wholesale tax reductions are out of the question if we are to maintain a balanced budget, and such tax reductions as we can afford must be applied in a way that will contribute most to the maintenance of employment.

The question is not so much one of incentives as of objectives. If we are to have a high level of national income, then, as I have indicated, we must have a high level of consumption outlays. The most important consideration, therefore, is that taxes should interfere as little as possible with the flow of consumer expenditures. The first step towards this end is to reduce indirect taxes on consumption and, if necessary, to substitute direct taxes on income. Indirect taxes are added to the price which the consumer must pay. The greater the sales tax, the fewer goods the customer can buy, and the less he can buy, the less the business man can sell. That, in turn, means less employment. At the same time, sales taxes penalize those who consume a large share of their income. There is thus a strong case for a drastic reduction in federal sales and excise taxes just as soon as the supply of consumer goods on the whole begins to exceed the demand. This condition is not likely to be reached until the backlog of deferred consumer demand has been met. The personal income tax should be the main source of federal revenue in the postwar period because it is the most flexible and equitable type of taxation, and because consumption is less affected by it.

Another important step in maintaining the flow of consumption expenditures would be to expand the social security program, including unemployment insurance, provision for old age, disability and other hazards. Coverage should be broadened, payments liberalized, and in the case of unemployment insurance, the period of payment should be lengthened. Providing an adequate old-age pension and extending it to cover everyone would enable a great many more people to retire, and this will assist in meeting the unemployment problem. Through provisions of this kind, a feeling of security is given to people generally and they are thus put in a position where they will feel free to spend a larger share of their current income, thereby contributing to the maintenance of employment.

Postwar tax policy will also have to be concerned with the flow of capital expenditures. In much of the current discussion, the deterrent effects of taxation upon business spending are exaggerated. Low taxes on business will not bring about a high level of capital expenditures if the demand for the products of business does not justify such expenditures. If demand does justify the expenditures, even high taxes will not keep businesses from expanding to meet the demand, unless they are subject to excessively high tax rates. The existence of markets for their products, rather than taxation, is the decisive factor, particularly in the case of large and well established enterprises, such as those in the steel, oil, automobile and chemical industries, among others. Present corporation tax laws have given considerable postwar protection to those concerns which have made excess profits by providing a postwar credit of 10 per cent of their excess profits tax, as well as a provision for the carry-back and carry-forward for two years of unused excess profits credits and of net operating losses. This is a tax incentive to business which already exists.

The effect of taxes on many of the small enterprises and on the establishment of new enterprises is another matter and needs to be given particular consideration. Perhaps the most important tax deterrent results from the fact that income is taxable under the corporation income tax, and it is again taxable under the personal income tax when it is distributed as dividends to the owners. This procedure has a number of harmful results. It places a premium on fixed debt financing and a penalty upon equity capital since the corporation may deduct interest as a cost item in computing its taxable income, while no such deduction is allowed for the return to stockholders on equity capital. It would greatly help to secure a less vulnerable business structure if more financing were done with equity capital and less with debt forms. Because of the existing situation, investors are reluctant to supply equity funds, particularly to small and new enterprises which are more risky than the larger, well-established enterprises. The personal income taxes upon dividends, particularly when subject to the higher surtaxes, are an inducement to stockholders with large incomes, who influence corporation policies, to prevent distribution of corporate earnings. This situation is likely to be detrimental to the maintenance of employment because corporations are thus led to retain earnings beyond what is needed and, therefore, they are not returned to the spending stream.

Equity investment and the distribution of corporate earnings would be greatly encouraged by adopting a plan somewhat similar to the British method of dealing with dividend income. One effective method would be to give a tax credit to the person who receives the dividends. A tax would be collected from the corporation as now, but when dividends are distributed, the stockholder would be permitted to take a credit on his personal income tax of some substantial fixed percentage of his dividend income. Another method would be to give the corporation a similar fixed percentage credit for that portion of its earnings which it distributes to stockholders. Either method would greatly reduce the amount of double taxation on equity capital and would be a strong incentive to new equity investments.

I think we should consider whether it would help in stabilizing the business structure to continue after reconversion some form of excess profits tax, together with more liberal provision for carry-forward and carry-back of the excess profits tax credit, and also make more liberal provision for carrying forward and carrying back losses than is now made in the tax law. Such provisions would be particularly helpful to small and new enterprises. We must encourage the establishment of new enterprises and safeguard the great number of existing small enterprises if we are to obtain a flexible and competitive business structure and halt the movement tending toward increasingly large combines and monopolies. Another most important step in this connection would be the establishment of patent pools freely available to small and new enterprises as well as to others.

There are numerous other problems, such as changes in the personal income tax which the limits of time do not permit me to consider. Our postwar tax structure must be flexible and adaptable to the changing requirements of fiscal policy. Tax policy must be recognized as part of a flexible fiscal system and must be used wisely to supplement or curtail the flow of consumer and business spending as conditions require.

Early Victory the Most Important Objective

Underlying all that I have said is the fundamental purpose of avoiding either inflation or deflation—in other words, what we would all like to have is full and sustained production and employment. The discussions before the Tax Institute—very properly—center around the role that taxation plays or should play in seeking this goal. I want to conclude what I have to say with this observation—nothing that can be done now or later to the tax structure, nothing that we can do now or later in any way, will contribute as much to the control of inflation—and what is infinitely more important, the saving of lives—as to unite all of our efforts and our energies to bring about victory in this war at the earliest possible moment. That is why I undertook to emphasize at the outset the overwhelming importance of keeping always in the forefront of our vision our duties now rather than our dollars later—for if we fail in the performance of our duties now, if we fail to do all that each of us individually and collectively as a nation can do to achieve an early victory, our plans and our hopes will never be realized.

CHAPTER XVIII

POSSIBILITIES OF POSTWAR INFLATION AND SUGGESTED TAX ACTION

J. W. Oliver

Secretary, Linen Thread Company, Inc.

When I was asked to prepare a paper on the possibilities of postwar inflation and suggested tax action, I was reminded of a cartoon by Mr. Galbraith entitled "Side Glances," where there was pictured a very enthusiastic woman talking to a sales clerk in a bookstore. The quoted remarks of the customer to the astonished bookseller are, "I want a book explaining military strategy, politics, OPA regulations, and inflation—not too big, to put in my handbag." This subject which I have been asked to discuss is so vast as to require not only one book, but numerous volumes; so I hope you will not be disappointed if I outline only the first draft of what might be called "a vest pocket edition."

Preceding speakers have dealt with inflation in the broader sense and their concept of inflation embraces more phases and ramifications than I shall attempt to cover. I propose to consider inflation primarily from the standpoint of there being a shortage of usable goods and services. The term "inflation," therefore, as I shall deal with it is relative.

If we have high prices with correspondingly high consumer income, that will not result in inflation, unless productivity fails to maintain its relative standing. Proceeding, therefore, from that relative point of view, I shall outline what I believe to be the required tax action necessary to stimulate production and thus avoid ruinous postwar inflation.

Recommendations for Postwar Tax Changes

The changes in the method of imposing taxes which should permit the proper flow of tax revenue to the federal treasury and, at the same time, stimulate productivity (or at least not constitute an anti-stimulus), may be summarized as follows:

1. Remove all taxes from corporations, excepting those constituting proper charges in computing cost of goods produced, or cost of services rendered.
2. Reduce the higher surtax rates on individual income tax to a point consistent with that which contemplates the greatest amount of revenue without seriously impeding the flow of venture capital into new or growing business.
3. Abolish capital gains taxes altogether and remove the question of capital gains or losses from all consideration of taxes.
4. Adopt a corporate tax policy somewhat along the lines of that existing in Great Britain before the war, that is, permit a reasonable withholding tax on corporate earnings as an advance payment on account of the shareholders. The individual in this instance should be allowed a deduction in computing his own taxes of the amount paid by the corporation on his behalf.
5. Retain the present penalty tax provision designed to avoid unnecessary accumulation of surplus; but change it if necessary to make it workable. I am suggesting no particular change, but I do realize that those who have had administrative experience with the current Act claim it to be unworkable. Surely, therefore, if we admit that the principle is correct, some means of changing the details so that accumulated surpluses held undistributed solely for the purpose of avoiding taxes, can be put to productive use, or the hoarding companies made to pay a proper cost for failure to make distribution.

Removal of Tax Upon Corporations

Now, let us enlarge upon the foregoing recommendations. I recognize that absolute equity in the matter of taxation is impossible of attainment. I am sure, however, that everyone in this audience will realize that the practice of imposing high taxes upon a corporation which are not credited to the individual at the time of distribution, goes a long way in complete disregard of the question of ability to pay. I frequently hark back to the principle enunciated by Adam Smith, who is often quoted as one of the first to advocate "taxation in accordance with ability to pay." While it is true that the cardinal principles of taxation advocated by Adam Smith included considerations other than ability to pay, it is absolutely inconsistent for those who quote him as their authority for having the man with the higher income pay more than proportionately higher taxes, still to advocate a high tax on corporations where thousands upon thousands of the stockholders are in the low income category. Why should the low income stockholder whose maximum tax rate is around 30 per cent, have his beneficial share of corporate earnings taxed at 60 per cent and then on the remaining 40 per cent at time of distribution be compelled to pay another 30 per cent?

Perhaps the framers of tax law in the past have been too much inclined to accept the terms "stockholders" and "wealthy individuals" as being one and the same, with the result that through their desire to soak the rich they have imposed an intolerable burden on many small stockholders. I will not burden you with any statistics purporting to show the proportion of corporate investments in the hands of the low or medium income classes, but I think you will agree that it is essential that these classes be encouraged to save; it is just as proper for them in the aggregate to own a substantial amount of corporate industry as it is to have war savings bonds widely held and in the hands of those who have the interest of our government at heart.

Business is only a medium through which industrial activity is carried out, and it is wrong to think in terms of "business," and especially "big business," as constituting something entirely apart from the other components of our economy.

Reduction of Higher Surtax Rates

With regard to the next suggestion, i.e., that the higher surtax rates be reduced, we must approach this phase of the problem from a standpoint of revenue. What constitutes the highest tax rate that will bring in the greatest amount of revenue and, at the same time, not act as an anti-stimulant to the flow of venture capital? We are dealing with a problem that perhaps can never be solved in the light of scientific accuracy. I am convinced, however, that somewhere down the line there is a point which could be considered the highest point of revenue productivity when you look at a long range of revenue flowing to the government, both as a result of current income and future income to be produced. You give me a competent man with a good picture of both the government and business side of the problem, who has the capability of a statistician and an actuary, and I will trust him to find that point, provided that his thinking is not distorted by preconceived notions of social reform; and further, provided that he is completely free of the domination of someone else who is motivated by the political outlook.

Removal of Capital Gains Taxes

As for the removal of the capital gains taxes, I am fully aware that instances can be cited where a man who enjoys capital gains has more ability to pay taxes than someone else. But we must look at the picture as a whole and think in terms of:

1. What is the present tax revenue from this source? And,

2. What are the potentialities of greater taxes on real income resulting from the releasing of stored up savings which otherwise may remain frozen?

While these questions must be taken into any consideration of capital gains taxes, they are, of course, also pertinent to the proper consideration of high surtaxes. Here, I think our reasoning is more likely to be warped by the consideration of an apparent advantage to the rich man than anything else. It takes real courage to advocate publicly a change that would constitute a "break" for the wealthy. But I believe it can be shown that the working class stand to gain more than anyone else by a change that would insure adequate capital for new and growing productive enterprises.

Adoption of British Corporate Tax Policy

The next suggestion has to do with a corporate tax policy along the lines existing in Great Britain prior to the war. I have in mind a plan whereby a reasonable tax, perhaps not much higher than the lowest surtax rate, would be imposed upon the earnings of a corporation in the year when earned. But it should be clearly understood that this is not a tax on the corporation in fact, but rather a temporary payment, temporarily treated as taxes, with the understanding that such amounts are to be credited to the stockholder when paying his taxes. The stockholder would be required to include the gross amount in his return of dividend income received.

Retention of Undistributed Earnings Tax

With regard to the suggestion that our present undistributed earnings tax provision remain in effect, possibly subject to minor changes, I feel that this is something to be worked out in the light of the individual circumstances surrounding each case. I hasten to say, however, that we should strive for simplicity and at any rate avoid administrative complications that would more than offset the advantage of the obtainable tax revenue. Perhaps there would be less necessity for this so-called penalty tax if the preceding suggestions were adopted. Personally, I dislike the use of tax provisions either to penalize or to offer incentives. I prefer to think in terms of a tax system that will accomplish the desired result in the most equitable manner and the necessary incentive to keep up a high rate of productivity to be a natural corollary of that well-rounded tax system. Success should be the reward of prudent investment and good management; and neither success nor failure should be traceable to ill-conceived tax legislation.

Congressional Tax Agency

You may be prompted to ask, "How would the foregoing be accomplished?" This, I admit, is more difficult. The solution of problems is more difficult that than of finding out what the problem is, but you can never solve a problem until you at least find out what you are trying to find out. Perhaps the surest way of reaching our goal would be to have Congress create an independent agency with full power to investigate all forms of tax law—both from the standpoint of governmental administration and taxpayer administration—which agency would be completely free of Congress and the Bureau of Internal Revenue, and its members would be appointed either for life, or a long term of office, with a sole function to investigate and recommend the best type of tax laws in the light of what the government must have on one hand, and the best interest of taxpayers at large on the other hand. I feel that such a board or agency should consist of men of the highest caliber obtainable, but be chosen so as to represent the government and taxpayers.

Such an agency might, to a considerable extent, take the place of the Ways and Means Committee in the Congress and the Finance Committee in the Senate. This agency would be relied upon to receive the recommendations or criticisms of all classes and all groups that now try to influence Congress in connection with the passage of revenue laws. It should be so constituted that both Congressmen and Senators could say to their constituents that they were largely governed by the recommendations of an unbiased body in determining the best tax law obtainable, for which reason neither the Congressmen nor the Senators would have to offer any apologies to their constituents. I do not mean to say that this body would have any legislative power, but I do mean to say that it should be of such high caliber that in ninety-nine chances out of one hundred the Congress would be willing to accept its recommendations. In addition to focusing tax policy with a view to obtaining the maximum release of economic power within the private sector of the economy, as well as meeting federal tax requirements, this agency should be entrusted with the problem of formulating a workable plan of coordinating state taxes and unifying them from a national point of view.

Unless the Congress can find a reasonable excuse not to listen to pressure groups, whether they represent business or labor unions, we will never have the type of tax legislation that should exist in this country. Therefore, I conclude that the first step toward any postwar planning which Congress should take with a view to adopting proper tax action in the light of possible postwar inflation, is that of creating an independent agency best able to deal with this problem. With that step taken, we should be on our way to a prosperous postwar era with little fear of inflation.

APPENDIX

TAX INFORMATION AND PUBLIC EDUCATION

APPENDIX

TAX INFORMATION AND PUBLIC EDUCATION

LEONARD POWER

Educational Consultant

ON THE SECOND afternoon of the Tax Institute Symposium in New York City on February 7 and 8, a group of educators and tax experts discussed what the schools could do to raise the general level of economic literacy, with particular emphasis on taxation.

The discussion was led by a panel of distinguished educators representing higher education, state departments of education, the United States Office of Education, the National Education Association, and the Association of School Business Officials. The purpose of the discussion was to pool experiences and to offer suggestions concerning what may be done to make school and college officials aware of present inadequacies and the need for creating an alert and informed public opinion in the field of civic education.

After some preliminary remarks by the various members of the panel, the discussion seemed to cluster about the following points:

1. It was recognized that there is a gap between the political level of taxation and the theoretically desirable level, and that education may help to reduce this gap. Dr. Frank W. Hubbard reported that the National Education Association, through its Committee on Taxation and School Finance, has selected six states in which to experiment in the reduction

of this gap by holding conferences on the state level, on regional levels within the states, and in selected localities. In these conferences educators and tax experts will meet with representatives of boards of education and of civic, business, and labor organizations. The reports of the first conferences to be held may be used to guide later conferences. A digest of the reports of several of these conferences may be published and distributed widely for use in other states. Although the primary purpose of this experiment is to explore the major problems of financing education, it is hoped that each conference and series of conferences will lead to a better understanding of the relationship of financing public education to the other public services of local and other governmental units. Dr. Edgar L. Morphet pointed out certain modifications in the tax structure of Florida that could be traced to the statewide study of taxation generated in educational circles and, for the most part, led by educators.

2. Educational leaders and lay leaders in each of the several fields, including the field of taxation, need to meet more often for the purpose of discussing common problems. It was pointed out that everybody is now more tax conscious than ever before, and that all of us are grasping for an understanding of the economic issues involved in world organization. The U. S. Office of Education reports that only five per cent of high school students are now receiving instruction in economics, not counting the excellent work in consumer economics courses for girls. There is need for laying a better foundational structure in the classrooms. But events are moving so rapidly that the immediate need is felt for a superstructure of less formal instruction.

At the adult level, much can be done through group meetings and by using the radio and the press. The planning of adult education is primarily an educational responsibility.

Information on governmental services and their costs can be prepared for publication by students in high schools. Students may also be used on radio programs but there is need for careful preparation of analyses and scripts, and it is at this point that the educators and tax experts should come together.

3. Citizenship in a democracy requires understanding on the part of the public of the local, state, and national tax policy. In their study of tax policies, educators should not limit their concern to the narrow area of the financial support of public education. It was pointed out that there is need for the cooperative development of standards by which educators and laymen may evaluate various tax proposals, since very little is now generally understood about the possible effects of proposed tax policies. The Tax Institute, other organizations interested in taxation, and educational organizations and associations at all levels should work together on the development of evaluative tax critera.

4. Although it takes fifty years to make a change in the school systems of the United States, the panel pointed out some first steps that may be taken without delay. One of these is the preparation by high school students of analyses and reports on local government budgets and expenditures—putting a premium upon graphic presentation of services and costs. The preparation of these reports, it was pointed out by Mr. Walter Millard of the Citizens Union, will help to give the students themselves a clear understanding of where the tax money goes. But in addition to such analyses and reports there is a definite need for high school study units on taxation. Little is now known by members of the panel of the extent to which such units have been developed. Professor Paul R. Mort pointed out that, even on the elementary school level, where all are reached by the schools, a beginning may be made through the subject of arithmetic. There is need for

further study and research regarding what is actually being done in the area in the public schools.

5. On the college level, and in the field of teacher preparation, the subject of taxation is sometimes included as a unit in a course on School Administration. Some institutions, notably Teachers College, Columbia University, Cornell, and the University of Michigan, are offering full courses on taxation to school superintendents, but few classroom teachers receive any training in this field.

Since the Tax Institute does not recommend tax policies, and since a panel discussion does not result in resolutions of any kind, the end results may be summarized by stating (1) that educators and tax experts enjoyed the opportunity afforded by the Tax Institute to come together; (2) that educators need to make greater use of the Tax Institute and other sources of tax information, and (3) that in the development of state, regional, and local educational or informational programs on taxation, tax experts should be regarded as essential resource persons for use in panel discussions, round tables, conferences, or institutes.

The members of the panel included: Professor Paul R. Mort, Teachers College, Columbia University; Roger M. Thompson, Director of Administration, Connecticut State Department of Education; Edgar L. Morphet, Consultant, Research and Statistics, U. S. Office of Education and Assistant State Superintendent of Florida Schools; Frank W. Hubbard, Director of Research, National Education Association; Edwin F. Nelson, Business Manager, Hartford, Connecticut Board of Education and President, Association of School Business Officials; and Leonard Power, Educational Consultant.

BIBLIOGRAPHY

It should be kept in mind that the following list of selected references does not purport to be a bibliography on war finance. Only such items have been included as appear to have a bearing on the theme of this volume, the curbing of inflation through taxation.

A few references relating to the first World War and to the postwar period which appear of significance in connection with the present situation have been included.

General

Crum, W. L., Fennelly, J. F., and Seltzer, L. H. *Fiscal Planning for Total War.* New York: National Bureau of Economic Research, 1942. 358 pp.

Fellner, William. *A Treatise on War Inflation.* Berkeley: University of California Press, 1942. 180 pp.

Haig, Robert Murray. *Financing Total War.* New York: Columbia University Press, 1942. 32 pp.

Harper, F. A., and Curtiss, W. M. "Inflation Is on Our Doorstep," *The Conference Board Economic Record* (July, 1943), 201-12.

Hart, Albert Gailord, and Allen, Edward D. *Paying for Defense.* Philadelphia: Blakiston Co., 1941. 275 pp.

Pigou, A. C. *The Political Economy of War.* New York: Macmillan Co., 1941. 169 pp.

Tax Institute. *Financing the War.* New York, 1942. 357 pp.

Wilcox, Clair. "Where Do We Stand on Inflation?" *The New York Times Magazine,* November 28, 1943.

Earmarks of Inflation

a. Retail Sales

Gilbert, Milton, and Jaszi, George. "National Income and National Product in 1942," *Survey of Current Business,* XXIII (March, 1943), 10-26.

Jaszi, George. "National Product and Income in the First Half of 1943," *Survey of Current Business,* XXIII (August, 1943), 9-14

Shelton, William C., and Beckler, Bernard. "Estimates of Sales of Retail Stores," *Survey of Current Business,* XXIII (November, 1943), 6-14.

b. Land Values

Anderson, Norris J. "Land Valuation in South Dakota," *Taxes—The Tax Magazine,* XX (1944), 158-60.

Cooper, Lee E. "Federal Agencies Seeking to Check Realty Inflation," *The New York Times,* January 9, 1944.

Federal Home Loan Bank Review. "Commissioner Fahey on Inflationary Lending." X (1943), 61.

——. "How Can Local Institutions Help to Stem the Tide of Over-Lending?" X (1944), 91-95.

GRAY, L. C., AND FLOYD, O. G. *Farm Land Values in Iowa.* Washington: United States Department of Agriculture. Bulletin 874. 1920.

HARDY, EDWARD K. "The Things That Are Bothering Property Owners These Days," *Mortgage Banker* (February, 1944), 1-2.

HOYT, HOMER. *One Hundred Years of Land Values in Chicago.* Chicago: University of Chicago Press, 1933. 519 pp.

JOHNSON, E. C. "The Farm Real Estate Market," *Federal Reserve Bulletin,* XXX (1944), 228-32.

JONES, ROLAND M. "Experts Warn of a Farm-Land Boom," *The New York Times,* March 12, 1944.

KELLOCK, HAROLD. "Agricultural Land Boom," *Editorial Research Reports,* I (February, 1944), 81-94.

MORSE, TRUE D. "Farm Land Boom or Boomerang," *Banking* (January, 1944), 47-49.

MORTGAGE BANKERS ASSOCIATION OF AMERICA. "Inflation in Real Estate—Is It Here or Coming?" *Mortgage Banker* (January, 1944), 1-3.

REGAN, M. M. "Are Farm Land Values Inflated?" *The Agricultural Situation,* XXVIII (April, 1944), 16-19.

c. *Savings*

LIVINGSTON, S. MORRIS. "Wartime Savings and Postwar Markets," *Survey of Current Business,* XXIII (September, 1943), 12-18.

WEILER, E. T. "Wartime Savings and Postwar Inflation," *Survey of Current Business,* XXIII (July, 1943), 13-18.

INFLATIONARY POTENTIALITIES OF THE PUBLIC DEBT

BURGESS, W. RANDOLPH. "Inflation and Its Relation to Government Loan Campaigns," *Proceedings of the Academy of Political Science.* New York, 1944. Pp. 3-8.

FAIRCHILD, FRED ROGERS. "The National Debt After the War," *Proceedings of the . . . National Tax Association, 1943.* Washington, 1944. Pp. 268-84.

HANSEN. ALVIN H. "Federal Debt Policy," *Proceedings of the . . . National Tax Association, 1943.* Washington, 1944. Pp. 256-67.

——. *Fiscal Policy and Business Cycles.* New York: W. W. Norton & Co., Inc., 1941. 462 pp.

——, AND PERLOFF, HARVEY S. *State and Local Finance in the National Economy.* Part III, "The Over-all Budget, Full Employment and Economic Stability," and Appendix A, "Moulton's 'The New Philosophy of Public Debt' ". New York: W. W. Norton & Co., Inc., 1944. Pp. 181-298.

KEITH, E. GORDON. "Borrowing and Inflation," *Financing the War.* New York: Tax Institute, 1942. Pp. 184-97.

KEMMERER, EDWIN W. *The ABC of Inflation.* New York: McGraw-Hill Book Co., 1942. 174 pp.

LELAND, SIMEON E. "Financing the War—Major Borrowing Policies," *Proceedings of the . . . National Tax Association,* 1943. Washington, 1944. Pp. 323-44.

MITNITZKY, MARK. "Some Monetary Aspects of Government Borrowing," *The American Economic Review,* XXXIII (1943), 21-37.

MOULTON, HAROLD G. *The New Philosophy of Public Debt.* Washington: Brookings Institution, 1943. 93 pp.

FISCAL DEVICES FOR CURBING INFLATION

BLOUGH, ROY. "Tax Policy and the Inflation Problem," *Proceedings of the . . . National Tax Association, 1942.* Washington, 1942. Pp. 298-305.

MAGILL, ROSWELL. "Inflation and Tax Policies," *Proceedings of the Academy of Political Science.* New York, 1944. Pp. 10-19.

PAUL, RANDOLPH E. "The Impact of Taxation on Consumer Spending," *Taxes—The Tax Magazine,* XXI (1943), 325-28.

SELTZER, LAWRENCE H. "Non-Revenue Objectives of Wartime Tax Policy," *Proceedings of the . . . National Tax Association, 1942.* Washington, 1942. Pp. 322-28.

SHOUP, CARL, FRIEDMAN, MILTON, AND MACK, RUTH P. *Taxing to Prevent Inflation.* New York: Columbia University Press, 1943. 236 pp.

TAX INSTITUTE. *Can We Raise $10 Billion in New Taxes in 1944?* Forum pamphlet. New York, 1943. 48 pp.

UNITED STATES CONGRESS, HOUSE. *Revenue Revision of 1943.* Hearings before Committee on Ways and Means, October 4-20, 1943. Washington: Government Printing Office, 1943. 1605 pp.

a. Sales Tax

BLAKEY, ROY G., AND BLAKEY, GLADYS C. "Federal Sales Tax or Spendings Tax," *Taxes—The Tax Magazine,* XXI (1943), 148-53, 183-84.

HARDY, CHARLES O. *Do We Want a Federal Sales Tax?* Washington: Brookings Institution, 1943. 47 pp.

LELAND, SIMEON E. "Income versus Sales Taxation as an Anti-Inflationary Control," *Financing the War.* New York: Tax Institute, 1942. Pp. 105-32.

LUTZ, HARLEY L. "The Sales Tax," *Bulletin of the National Tax Association,* XXIX (1944), 112-15.

SHULTZ, WILLIAM J. "Economic Effects of a Federal General Sales Tax," *Taxes—The Tax Magazine,* XXI (1943), 419-21.

UNITED STATES TREASURY DEPARTMENT. "Considerations Respecting a Federal Retail Sales Tax," *Revenue Revision of 1943.* Hearings before the Committee on Ways and Means, October, 1943. Washington: Government Printing Office, 1943. Pp. 1095-1272.

b. Spendings Tax

BUEHLER, ALFRED G. "Taxation of Consumer Expenditures," *Proceedings of the . . . National Tax Association, 1942.* Washington, 1942. Pp. 260-64.

——. "Taxing Consumer Spending," *Bulletin of the National Tax Association,* XXVIII (1943), 123-28.

FISHER, IRVING, AND FISHER, HERBERT W. *Constructive Income Taxation.* New York: Harper & Bros., 1942. 277 pp.

FRIEDMAN, MILTON. "The Spendings Tax as a Wartime Fiscal Measure," *The American Economic Review,* XXXIII (1943), 50-62.

HAENSEL, PAUL. "The Spendings Tax and the Victory Tax," *Taxes—The Tax Magazine,* XX (1942), 614-19.

HARRISS, C. LOWELL. "Revenue Implications of a Progressive-Rate Tax on Expenditures," *The Review of Economic Statistics,* XXV (1943), 175-91.

MARSH, DONALD B. "Wartime Fiscal Policy," *Taxes—The Tax Magazine,* XXII (1944), 104-8.

MORGENTHAU, HENRY. Statement to Senate Finance Committee, September 3, 1942. Washington: Treasury Department, 1942. 5 pp.

PAUL, RANDOLPH E. Memorandum to Ways and Means Committee, June 22, 1942. 6 pp. Statement to Senate Finance Committee, September 3, 1942. 8 pp. Supplementary Statement. 2 pp. Washington: Treasury Department, 1942.

POOLE, KENYON E. "Problems of Administration and Equity Under a Spendings Tax," *The American Economic Review,* XXXIII (1943), 63-73.

TAX INSTITUTE. "A Spendings Tax," *Tax Policy,* IX (1942), 1-6.

WALLIS, W. ALLEN. "How to Ration Consumers' Goods and Control Their Prices," *The American Economic Review,* XXXII (1942), 501-12.

c. Excises

CLINE, DENZEL C. "General Sales Taxes and Selective Excises," *Financing the War.* New York: Tax Institute, 1942. Pp. 75-92.

CRAIG, DAVID R. "Excise Taxes to Control Consumption," *Proceedings of the . . . National Tax Association,* 1941. Washington, 1941. Pp. 751-56.

PETTENGILL, ROBERT B. "Classified versus Selected Sales Taxes to Finance the Defense Program," *Proceedings of the . . . National Tax Association, 1941.* Washington, 1941. Pp. 736-42.

TAX INSTITUTE. "Wrestling With Excises," *Tax Policy,* VIII (1941), 3-11.

WALKER, MABEL L. "Revenue Possibilities of Federal Excises and General Sales Taxes," *Proceedings of the . . . National Tax Association, 1941.* Washington, 1941. Pp. 742-46.

d. Individual Income Tax

COMSTOCK, ALZADA. "Role of Income and Profits Taxes in the Control of Inflation," *Financing the War.* New York: Tax Institute, 1942. Pp. 93-104.

HART, ALBERT GAILORD. "Income Taxation in War Finance," *Proceedings of the . . . National Tax Association,* 1942. Washington, 1942. Pp. 220-29.

LUTZ, HARLEY L. "A Tax on Gross Income Payments to Individuals," *Financing the War.* New York: Tax Institute, 1942. Pp. 133-55.

PAUL, RANDOLPH E. "The Income Tax in Total War," *Proceedings of the . . . National Tax Association,* 1942. Washington, 1942. Pp. 244-52.

e. Forced Savings

JÈZE, GASTON. *Cours de Science des Finances et de Législation Financière Française.* Paris: Giard, 1922. 6th ed. Vol. II. Pp. 490-502.

KEYNES, JOHN MAYNARD. *How to Pay for the War.* New York: Harcourt, Brace and Co., 1940. 88 pp.

LOTZ, W. "Forced Savings," *Encyclopedia of the Social Sciences, 1931.* Vol. VI. Pp. 346-47.

PATCH, BUEL W. "Forced Savings," *Editorial Research Reports,* II (September, 1942), 187-200.

TAX INSTITUTE. "Forced Savings," *Tax Policy,* IX (1942), 3-10.

UNITED STATES LIBRARY OF CONGRESS, DIVISION OF BIBLIOGRAPHY. *Forced Savings: a List of References.* Compiled by Grace H. Fuller. Washington, 1942. 20 pp.

WEST, E. E. "The Validity of Forced Loans in Time of War: a Consideration of S. 1650," *George Washington Law Review*, VIII (1940), 904-28.

f. Social Security Taxes

HARRIS, S. E. *Economics of Social Security Taxes.* New York: McGraw-Hill Book Co., 1941. 455 pp.

HART, ALBERT GAILORD. "Forced Loans and Social Security Taxes as Inflation Remedies," *Financing the War.* New York: Tax Institute, 1942. Pp. 156-67.

EXPERIENCE OF OTHER COUNTRIES IN CURBING INFLATION THROUGH FISCAL DEVICES

BLODGETT, RALPH H. "Public Finance," *Comparative Economic Systems.* New York: Macmillan Co., 1944. Pp. 513-41.

MUSGRAVE, R. A. "The Wartime Tax Effort of the United States, the United Kingdom, and Canada," *Federal Reserve Bulletin,* XXX (1944), 16-27.

a. Russia

HAENSEL, PAUL. "Recent Changes in the Soviet Tax System," *Taxes—The Tax Magazine,* XIX (1941), 677-82.

——. "The 1943 Tax Increases in U.S.S.R." *Bulletin of the National Tax Association,* XXIX (1944), 167-69.

LOUCKS, WILLIAM N. "Economic Planning; the State Budget," *Comparative Economic Systems.* New York: Harper & Bros. Pp. 499-583.

b. Italy

FOA, B. G., AND TREVES, P. G. "Italian Finance and Investment," *Economica,* VI, New Series (1939), 270-95.

"LANFRANCUS" (F.M.T.). "La politica finanziaria del governo fascista (1936-1941)," *Quaderni Italiana,* I (January, 1942). Boston.

c. Canada

BROWN, F. H., GIBSON, J. D., AND PLUMPTRE, A. F. W. *War Finance in Canada.* Toronto: The Ryerson Press, 1940. 110 pp.

CANADA. MINISTER OF FINANCE. *Annual Budget Speeches, 1939-43.* Ottawa: Department of Finance.

EATON, A. B. "Canadian Tax Policy and National Pricing Policy," *Proceedings of the . . . National Tax Association, 1942.* Washington, 1942. Pp. 314-21.

STIKEMAN, H. HEWARD. "Canadian Experience in Financing the War," *Proceedings of the . . . National Tax Association, 1943.* Washington, 1944. Pp. 345-59.

WYNNE, WILLIAM H. "Canadian War Finance," *Financing the War.* New York: Tax Institute, 1942. Pp. 284-98.

d. Great Britain

BATHURST, M. E. "The Incidence of Taxation in Britain," *Taxes—The Tax Magazine,* XXI (1943), 602-13.

BRITISH INFORMATION SERVICES. *Direct Taxation and Post-War Credits in Britain.* New York, 1943. 7 pp.

——. *The British War Savings Campaign.* New York, 1943. 6 pp.

——. *The Burden of Taxation in Britain.* New York, 1943. 12 pp.

GREAT BRITAIN. CHANCELLOR OF THE EXCHEQUER. *Financial Statements. 1939-44.* London: H. M. Stationery Office.

GREAT BRITAIN. TREASURY. *An Analysis of the Sources of War Finance and an Estimate of the National Income and Expenditure in 1938, 1940, 1941, and 1942.* London: H. M. Stationery Office. Cmd. 6261, Cmd. 6347, and Cmd. 6438.

——. *A New System for the Taxation of Weekly Wage Earners.* London: H. M. Stationery Office, 1943. Cmd. 6469.

——. *The Taxation of Weekly Wage Earners.* London: H. M. Stationery Office, 1942. Cmd. 6348. 16 pp.

HILL, WALTER. "Britain's 'Pay-As-You-Go' Plan," *Taxes—The Tax Magazine,* XXI (1943), 649-50.

KALDOR, NICHOLAS. "The 1941 White Paper on National Income and Expenditure," *Economic Journal,* LII (1942), 206-22.

——. "The 1943 White Paper on National Income and Expenditure," *Economic Journal,* LIII (1943), 259-74.

MURPHY, MARY E. *The British War Economy.* New York: Professional & Technical Press, 1943. 403 pp.

SHIRRAS, G. FINDLAY, AND ROSTAS, L. *The Burden of British Taxation.* New York: Macmillan Co., 1943. 240 pp.

THOMAS, BRINLEY. "How Britain is Avoiding Inflation," *Financing the War.* New York: Tax Institute, 1942. Pp. 269-83.

POSSIBILITIES OF POSTWAR INFLATION AND SUGGESTED TAX ACTION

CONNOLLY, JOHN L. "Business Suggestions for Improving Tax Policy," *Proceedings of the . . . National Tax Association, 1943.* Washington, 1944. Pp. 426-34.

EINZIG, PAUL. *World Finance, 1914-1935.* Part I, "Inflation." New York: Macmillan Co., 1935. Pp. 15-98.

MAGILL, ROSWELL. *The Post War Federal Tax System.* New York: Tax Foundation, 1943. 12 pp.

RICHES, E. J., AND JACK, L. B. "The Transition from War to Peace Economy," *International Labour Review,* XLVIII (1943), 1-22.

RUML, BEARDSLEY. "A Postwar National Fiscal Program," *The New Republic,* LX (1944), 265-68.

SELIGMAN, EDWIN R. A. *Essays in Taxation.* "The War Revenue Acts," "Loans versus Taxes in War Finance," and "The Cost of the War and How It Was Met." New York: Macmillan Co., 1931. Pp. 679-782.

——. *Studies in Public Finance.* "Comparative Tax Burdens in the Twentieth Century," and "Fiscal Reconstruction." New York: Macmillan Co., 1925. Pp. 1-43, 204-24.

SHULTZ, WILLIAM J., AND CAINE, M. R., *Financial Development of the United States.* "Inflation," and "Deflation." New York: Prentice-Hall, Inc., 1937. Pp. 564-72.

SIMONS, HENRY. "Postwar Federal Tax Reform," *Proceedings of the . . . National Tax Association,* 1943. Washington, 1944. Pp. 434-43.

INDEX